SOCIAL SECURITY STRATEGIES

WILLIAM REICHENSTEIN
AND WILLIAM MEYER

D0188035

Copyright © 2011 by William Reichenstein and William Meyer. All rights reserved.

No part of this publication may be reproduced, stored in a retrieval system, or transmitted in any form or by any means, electronic, mechanical, photocopying, recording, or otherwise, without prior written permission from the authors.

Information in this book is accurate at the time of publication and is based on the policies and promises of the Social Security system at the time of publication. However, the policies of the Social Security system can be changed at any time. Readers should evaluate the applicability of any recommendation in this publication in light of the policies and promises in effect at the time of reading.

Limit of Liability/Disclaimer of Warranty: Every effort has been made to ensure this publication is as accurate and complete as possible. However, no representations or warranties are made with respect to the accuracy or completeness of the contents of this book. It is not the intent of this publication or its authors to provide professional tax, investment or legal advice. The strategies contained herein may not be suitable for your situation. You should consult with a professional where appropriate. This publication should be used only as a general guideline and not as the ultimate source of information about Social Security claiming strategies.

The purpose of this publication is to educate. The authors shall have neither liability nor responsibility to any person or entity with respect to any loss or damage caused, or alleged to be caused, directly or indirectly, by information contained in this publication.

ISBN: 978-0-615-45753-6

Library of Congress Control Number: 2011924959

Printed in the United States of America

Acknowledgements

We thank the following people from the Social Security Administration for their help in answering our numerous questions: Dorothy Clark, Senior Public Affairs Specialist, National Press Office, Wes Davis, Regional Communications Director, Dallas, Texas, and his associate Aurora Arias-Lopez, and Gloria Walker of the Waco, Texas, office of Social Security Administration. We thank Darlene Oldendick, a retired Social Security agent, for her helpful comments and insights. In addition, we thank Robin Brewton and Charlie Ryan of Social Security Solutions, Inc. for edits and suggestions on content that materially improved the book.

Request for Feedback

Our research, writing and education on effective claiming strategies will continue beyond the publication of this book, and as changes to Social Security unfold, new claiming strategies will undoubtedly evolve. We invite readers to share feedback with us. How have you been able to use the information in this book? Have you created strategies in addition to those here that you believe others would benefit from? Have you been able to craft a strategy in a particular situation that made a material difference for a client?

We've established an email address for receiving your feedback about this book and the strategies you've created: ReaderCommunity@SocialSecuritySolutions.com. Through this email address you can become a member of our reader community dedicated to enhancing Americans' understanding of Social Security retirement benefits. We will provide to community members periodic updates on claiming strategies, invitations to learning events, opportunities to share with other members, and exclusive offers for new or enhanced tools. We will not share information you provide without your expressed consent to do so.

About the Authors

Dr. William Reichenstein is Social Security Solutions, Inc.'s Director of Research. Bill currently holds the Pat and Thomas R. Powers Chair in Investment Management at Baylor University. He has taught and researched in finance since 1978, with his recent work concentrating on the interaction between investments and taxes. He has written more than 150 articles for professional and academic journals. He is a frequent contributor to *Journal of Financial Planning, Journal of Investing, Financial Analysts Journal, Journal of Portfolio Management,* and *Journal of Wealth Management,* and is frequently quoted in the *Wall Street Journal* and elsewhere. He earned a BA in math from St. Edward's University and a Ph.D. in economics from the University of Notre Dame. He is a Chartered Financial Analyst (CFA).

William Meyer is the founder of Social Security Solutions, Inc., and the creator of the Social Security Strategy Analyzer software tool. In recognizing the void that has existed for personalized and pragmatic advice related to Social Security at retirement, Bill founded Social Security Solutions, Inc. based on his expertise and that of Dr. William Reichenstein, Social Security Solutions, Inc.'s Head of Research. Bill Meyer is an expert in Social Security and the retirement industry and is committed to helping Baby Boomers make the most of their retirement savings. His career in wealth management spans Charles Schwab, H&R Block and Advisor Software Inc. He earned his Bachelor of Science degree in Psychology from UCLA and his MBA degree from the Anderson School at UCLA. He is a former Trustee of the Securities Industry Institute at Wharton and holds multiple securities licenses.

Both Reichenstein and Meyer are recognized experts on Social Security claiming strategies. They have published numerous articles about the subject, and have been quoted in publications such as *SmartMoney*, *Forbes*, *Barron's*, the *Wall Street Journal* and the *Chicago Tribune*. In March of 2010, their research entitled "Social Security: When you Should Start Benefits and How to Minimize Longevity Risk," was published in the *Journal of Financial Planning*.

Contents

Setting the Context

For many retirees, Social Security benefits represent their largest financial asset. Unfortunately, most Americans decide when to begin Social Security benefits without any advice. Yet, for many Americans, it represents their largest financial asset. Representatives at the Social Security Administration are not allowed to give advice (even if asked) and can only provide information and details on the rules. And few advisors have the training and knowledge to help a retiree select a Social Security claiming strategy.

The largest and smartest banks and financial institutions do not train their advisors to provide advice about when to begin Social Security benefits. These institutions have not succeeded in creating a way to earn revenue for providing advice on Social Security claiming strategies. As a result, they do not provide education for their advisors who, in turn, cannot provide quality advice to clients.

A majority of Americans have no idea how important selecting a Social Security claiming strategy can be. A smart claiming strategy can often mean hundreds of thousands of dollars in added benefits over a retiree's lifetime. Yet, research from The Financial Literacy Center in 2010 illustrates that American retirees are both unaware of the magnitude of the decisions surrounding claiming retirement benefits and, more importantly, are unqualified to make decisions about their benefits.[1]

---

1 "Framing Effects and Claiming Behavior of Social Security," Financial Literacy Center, October 2010; "What Do People Know About Social Security," Financial Literacy Center, October 2010; "How Much Do People Know About Social Security," Financial Literacy Center, November 2010.

Billions of dollars in lifetime benefits are lost each year because retirees make poor choices about when to begin their benefits. In 2009, consistent with previous years, 74% of all Social Security claimants started benefits before Full Retirement Age.[2] For some, that was the right decision based on factors you will read about in this book. But for most, claiming early was not their best strategy. For this collective group, starting benefits early will result in billions of dollars in reduced lifetime benefits compared to having selected a claiming strategy that maximizes their benefits and provides the best income solution to their unique situation.

2 "Annual Statistical Supplement to the Social Security Bulletin," Social Security Administration, released February 2010.

CHAPTER 1 Introduction

Today, perhaps more than any other time since the inception of Social Security in 1935, retirees are more dependent on America's retirement entitlement program. Unfortunately, the rules and calculations surrounding a person's Social Security benefits are complicated. We have written this book as a guide to creating a personalized and smart Social Security claiming strategy. Our book is directed primarily to financial advisors who counsel retirees. These advisors include financial planners, CFAs, tax professionals from CPAs to Enrolled Agents, attorneys, and others managing private wealth or providing advice to retirees and pre-retirees. However, individuals can also benefit from this book. We provide a broad analysis of the factors that ultimately impact the amount of collected benefits. Depending on marital status, age, projected lifetime, and other factors, one can create a smart claiming strategy that may significantly increase cumulative lifetime benefits. We also discuss other strategies that may better fit unique situations. The bottom line is that every year millions of Americans claim benefits in a suboptimal way, leaving billions of dollars on the table that could bolster their standard of living in retirement.

Definition of Social Security Claiming Strategy

A Social Security claiming strategy refers to a decision as to when a single individual will begin his or her benefits or when each partner of a couple will begin their own benefits and, when applicable, their spousal benefits.

The best claiming strategy considers the rules and constraints of the Social Security system. In addition, it considers:

(1) Projected cumulative lifetime benefits, and

(2) How the claiming strategy would affect the projected longevity of the financial assets.

What does this mean? For any individual or couple, there are numerous factors that can impact the amount of their expected cumulative lifetime benefits. Factors such as the relative ages of each spouse and their expected longevities can materially affect projected cumulative lifetime benefits. Yet few retirees consider these factors in their planning. To create an optimal strategy, benefit projections for each set of applicable factors must be analyzed. We provide side-by-side comparisons of projected benefits from competing claiming strategies. These comparisons allow individuals to see the tradeoffs of alternative strategies and thus make informed decisions when selecting their claiming strategy. This book will illustrate the rubrics and principles for constructing and evaluating strategies.

Why Is This Topic Important?

It is no secret that millions of Americans are unprepared for retirement. The flat stock market from 2000-2009, with market meltdowns in 2000-2002 and 2007-2008, has adversely affected the financial preparedness of millions of pre-retirees. Financial losses associated with retirement savings and job losses among those approaching retirement have significantly impacted pre-retirees and recent retirees. Corporations are discontinuing defined-benefit pensions, thus pushing the responsibility of funding retirement to individuals. Finally, we have seen savings rates dwindle across generations with the result that many Baby Boomers are financially unprepared for retirement. The culmination of these factors—(1) low retirement savings, (2) reduced availability of defined benefit pension plans, and (3) the financial market meltdowns—mean that Social Security benefits represent a larger portion of many Americans' retirement nest eggs than perhaps ever before.

An April 2010 Gallup poll article entitled "Americans Shift Expectations About Retirement Funding," suggests that many retirees are more dependent on Social Security than previous generations. According to the Social Security Administration, in 2010 Social Security benefits replaced about 40% of the average retiree's income in retirement. This percentage ranges from over 51% for low income families to 28% for families earning the maximum income covered by Social Security. While these statistics are interesting, the key point is that everyone should strive to select a Social Security claiming strategy that is best for their situation. The right claiming strategy may maximize their projected cumulative lifetime benefits and ensure adequate income should they live a long life. From a financial planning perspective, crafting an optimal claiming strategy can reduce the risk that the client will outlive his financial resources. For Americans, a smart Social Security claiming strategy can increase their standard of living and maximize benefits for a surviving spouse. Most Americans make this critical claiming decision without understanding the rules governing benefits or without advice from someone who can help them make an informed claiming decision. Unfortunately, a poor claiming decision can permanently reduce a retiree's standard of living and increase the probability that he will outlive his resources and be a financial burden to his children.

Potential Changes in Social Security Promises

The recommended strategies in this book are based on the current promises of the Social Security system. Obviously, there will be changes made to this system. However, we join others who believe these changes will likely have little, if any, impact on current retirees and those now approaching retirement. Consequently, the recommendations in this book should prove useful for this book's target audience.

Social Security is not going broke in the near future. Actuarial projections predict that tapping just the interest from the Old-Age and Survivors Insurance (OASI) trust fund will support all benefits through 2024, and tapping the remaining principal from the trust fund is expected to provide funding for all benefits through 2037.

As previously noted, many individuals claim Social Security benefits as soon as possible. One argument frequently given by these individuals for beginning benefits early is they want to get what they can before the system goes broke. We believe this is a poor reason to begin benefits early. Although no one knows how the system may change, opinions of several groups suggest that potential changes for Americans age 55 or older would likely be minimal. For example, Boston College's Center for Retirement Research publishes "The Social Security Claiming Guide," which can be accessed at crr.bc.edu/social_security_guide. One section of this Guide states without qualification, "Don't start [benefits] early because Social Security has money problems. ... You won't get more if you do." It also states, "Nearly all proposals to fix Social Security would also protect those age 55 and older." We agree with these opinions.

Several other publications also discuss potential changes to Social Security. "The Social Security Claiming Guide," "The Social Security Fix-It Book," and Thomas N. Bethell in his article "Social Security: Where Do We Go From Here?" all offer perspectives of possible changes and their impacts.[1] Potential changes discussed in these sources include raising the Full Retirement Age for people born after 1960, linking benefits for earnings in years before age 60 to inflation instead of the average wage level, raising payroll taxes, earmarking estate tax revenue for Social Security, and diversifying the Social Security trust fund to include stocks. None of these changes would materially affect projected Social Security benefits for people older than 55.

Separately, Paul Ryan, a member of both the House Budget Committee and the Deficit Commission, introduced drafted legislation to reduce

---

1 See crr.bc.edu/special_projects/the_social_security_fix-it_book.html and Thomas N. Bethell, "Social Security: Where Do We Go from Here?" *AARP Bulletin*, July-August 2010, 16-19.

the Social Security deficit in "A Roadmap for America's Future." It would reduce future Social Security benefits for workers who are 55 or younger in 2011, but lock in benefits for workers over 55. When asked about the Roadmap, House Majority Leader Eric Cantor said "the starting point in any plan ... has got to be, we need to distinguish between those at or nearing retirement. Anyone 55 or older in this country has got to know that their Social Security benefits ... will not be changed."[2]

In short, changes will occur in the Social Security system. But we join others who believe that these changes will likely have little, if any, impact on individuals in or near retirement. Therefore, the advice in this book should prove useful for this target audience.

Constructing Smart Strategies

While researching and writing this book, we were challenged by the nuances and multitude of rules governing Social Security retirement benefits. Our mission is to devise strategies and heuristics that help people assimilate all the pieces in order to analyze, compare and ultimately decide on a claiming strategy. The rules are voluminous and, at times, hard to interpret. Together they are complicated, and what may seem like an intuitive strategy along one dimension may actually be flawed when all the applicable factors are considered. The most significant deficiency we see, and the one we hope to eliminate with this publication, is the lack of a resource that presents these rules together with advice on how to select a claiming strategy. All of these rules must be considered in concert when recommending or selecting a claiming strategy. Spousal benefits and survivor's benefits serve as good examples of this. It's simple to calculate how a husband's decision as to when to begin benefits based on his earnings record will affect his benefits. But his decision should also consider how his beginning date will affect his wife's spousal benefits and, potentially, her survivor's benefits. Spousal and survivor's benefits can add hundreds of thousands of dollars in lifetime benefits. Putting everything together requires careful planning.

2 See "Obama won't back Social Security Reform," Washington Post, Jan 25, 2011.

Finally, we have developed a complementary software tool that uses the techniques outlined in this book. This tool was developed in two versions: one with a simple interface for consumers, and the other with more sophisticated diagnostics for financial advisors and practitioners. Additionally, we have published related detailed research in academic journals and have more research in progress. Readers who are interested in the tool and additional research should review information at www.SocialSecuritySolutions.com or www.RetireeIncome.com. The authors of this book formed the firm that developed these websites and the complementary software tool.

In conclusion, if you are an individual consumer wanting to learn more about your Social Security benefit choices, we are your Social Security advocate. We will help you construct a smart claiming strategy. If you are an advisor, our goal is to help you construct smart strategies for your clients. Social Security is an important component of retirement planning. Unfortunately, it is also complex. Social Security benefit planning must be approached with an analytical mind-set. A good claiming strategy must reflect the client's specific situation. In addition, the client should be able to compare one strategy against another. A good claiming strategy can enhance a client's retirement lifestyle and reduce the chances that he will deplete his financial resources in retirement.

CHAPTER 2	Defining Social Security Terms

There are a few key terms that are important in crafting Social Security strategies. While not exciting to read, an understanding of the key terms is critical in order to understand the role certain factors play in creating an overall strategy. This chapter explains the key terms related to Social Security. These terms will appear throughout the book and will be in bold type the first time each appears. Readers already familiar with these terms and their implications to Social Security benefits may want to use this chapter as a reference when needed. Key terms covered in this chapter are Full Retirement Age, Primary Insurance Amount, delayed retirement credits, bend points, and Average Indexed Monthly Earnings

Full Retirement Age

Full Retirement Age (FRA) is the age at which an individual receives the full retirement benefit from Social Security. It is sometimes called **Normal Retirement Age**. People who begin benefits at Full Retirement Age receive their **Primary Insurance Amount**. The FRA for individuals varies by birth year.

Before explaining FRA in more detail, we first must discuss two caveats to the term. First, for some unknown reason, Social Security rules consider people to attain an age the day before their birthday. Consequently, someone born on January 1, 1945, actually is considered to be age 66 on December 31, 2010, the day before his 66th birthday. Also, he has the Full Retirement Age for someone born in 1944, the day before his actual birthday.

Someone born on January 1, 1955, has the Full Retirement Age for someone born in 1954. Second, each individual has an FRA for benefits based on her earnings record and for her spousal benefits, but she may have a different FRA for survivor's benefits. When deciding when to begin Social Security benefits, the FRA for your own benefits and spousal benefits is the key factor. Therefore, unless otherwise stated, when we mention FRA in this book, we are referring to the FRA for "own" benefits (a.k.a., benefits based on your earnings record, worker's benefits) and spousal benefits, but not survivor's benefits.

Now that these caveats have been explained, let's look at FRAs for worker's benefits and spousal benefits by year of birth. From Table 2.1, for someone born in 1941 and 1942, FRA is 65 years and eight months and 65 years and ten months, respectively. It is 66 for someone born from 1943 to 1954. It is 66 years and two months for someone born in 1955, and the FRA rises by two months per year through 1959. For someone born in 1960 or later, FRA is 67.

Someone who begins benefits at Full Retirement Age (FRA) receives full benefits, that is, the **Primary Insurance Amount**. Someone who begins benefits before attaining FRA receives reduced benefits, while someone who delays benefits until after FRA receives a higher level of benefits. Table 2.1 shows the reductions in benefits for starting Social Security benefits before attaining FRA and the increase in benefits for delaying the start of benefits until after FRA.

Table 2.1.	Social Security Eligibility: Ages for Full Retirement Benefits for Your Own and Spousal Benefits, and Reductions and Credits for Early and Delayed Benefits				
Year of Birth*	Full Re-tirement Age (FRA)	Per Month Reduction if Benefits Begin Prior to Full Retirement Age	Age 62 Benefits as a % of PIA	Per Month Delayed Retire-ment Credits	Age 70 Benefits as % of PIA
1941	65 and 8 mos	5/9% for 36 mos.+5/12%/mo.**	76 2/3%	0.625%	132 ½%
1942	65 and 10 mos	5/9% for 36 mos. +5/12%/mo.**	75 5/6%	0.625%	131 ¼%
1943-54	66	5/9% for 36 mos. +5/12%/mo.**	75%	2/3%	132%
1955	66 and 2 mos	5/9% for 36 mos.+5/12%/mo.**	74 1/6%	2/3%	130 2/3%
1956	66 and 4 mos	5/9% for 36 mos.+5/12%/mo.**	73 1/3%	2/3%	129 1/3%
1957	66 and 6 mos	5/9%for 36 mos.+5/12%/mo.**	72 ½%	2/3%	128%
1958	66 and 8 mos	5/9% for 36 mos.+5/12%/mo.**	71 2/3%	2/3%	126 2/3%
1959	66 and 10 mos	5/9% for 36 mos.+5/12%/mo.**	70 5/6%	2/3%	125 1/3%
1960 or later	67	5/9% for 36 mos.+5/12%/mo.**	70%	2/3%	124%

*Social Security considers people born on January 1 to have been born in the prior year.
**The monthly reduction is 5/9% for the first 36 months prior to Full Retirement Age, and 5/12% for every month after the first 36 months.

The reductions and increases for someone with an FRA of 66 are important because this affects most individuals who will be deciding when to begin Social Security benefits in the next several years. If this individual begins Social Security benefits before attaining FRA, the reduction is 5/9% per month for the first 36 months plus 5/12% per month for months 37 through 48. So, if benefits are begun at 62, 63, 64, or 65, the reduction is 25%,

20%, 13.33%, and 6.67%, respectively, below the Primary Insurance Amount. If benefits are begun at 63 years and one month, then the reduction is 19.44%, where the latter is 35 months times 5/9% reduction per month.

If benefits are begun after FRA, the increase is 2/3% per month for each month benefits are delayed until age 70. So, if benefits are begun at 67, 68, 69, or 70, the increases in benefits—called **delayed retirement credits**—are 8%, 16%, 24%, and 32%, respectively, above the Primary Insurance Amount. If benefits are begun three months after attaining FRA, then the delayed retirement credit is 2%, [3 months times 2/3% per month]. So, the monthly benefits level is 102% of PIA. This example and a prior one emphasize that someone does not need to wait a full year (e.g. from 63 to 64 or 66 to 67) to get a higher benefit amount. The benefit amount increases each month that benefits are delayed from age 62 to 70.

For someone with an FRA of 66 and Primary Insurance Amount of $1,000, the levels of benefits if started at 62 through 70 would be $750 at 62, $800, $866, $933, $1,000 at 66, $1,080, $1,160, $1,240, and $1,320 at 70.[3] All amounts are adjusted for annual **Cost of Living Adjustments** (COLAs). The Date Issues section of Chapter 5 explains how the Social Security Administration counts months for the reduction period and for delayed retirement credits.

Table 2.2 presents the Full Retirement Ages for survivor's benefits. This FRA also adopts the caveat whereby someone born on January 1 is considered to have been born in the prior year. For survivor's benefits, the FRA is 66 years and two months for someone born in 1957, and it rises by two months per year through 1962. For someone born in 1962 or later, it is age 67.

---

3 In practice, all monthly benefits are rounded down to the next lowest dollar if not already a whole dollar. For example, benefits at age 64 would be $866 for someone with a PIA of $1,000, but $1,733 for someone with a PIA of $2,000. In this book, we generally ignore this rounding.

Table 2.2.	Full Retirement Ages for Survivor's Benefits for Widow(er)s Born after 1939

If your birth date is...	Then your full retirement age is...
1/2/40-1/1/41	65 years and 2 months
1/2/41-1/1/42	65 years and 4 months
1/2/42-1/1/43	65 years and 6 months
1/2/43-1/1/44	65 years and 8 months
1/2/44 1/1/45	65 years and 10 months
1/2/45-1/1/57	66 years
1/2/57-1/1/58	66 years and 2 months
1/2/58-1/1/59	66 years and 4 months
1/2/59-1/1/60	66 years and 6 months
1/2/60-1/1/61	66 years and 8 months
1/2/61-1/1/62	66 years and 10 months
1/2/62 and later	67 years

Source: http://www.ssa.gov/OP_Home/handbook/handbook.07\handbook-0723.html

The FRA *for all benefits* is 66 for people born between 1945 and 1954, and this group includes most people that will be deciding when to begin Social Security benefits in the next several years.

Primary Insurance Amount

Primary Insurance Amount (PIA) is the level of monthly Social Security benefits if begun at the individual's Full Retirement Age. If Social Security benefits have already begun, they will continue at their current level subject only to the annual Cost of Living Adjustment. Consequently, this discussion may be of little importance to those individuals. If benefits have not yet begun, then ***Your Retirement Benefit Estimate*** provides an estimate of an individual's PIA. The *Your Retirement Benefit Estimate*, which is discussed in Appendix 2A at the end of this chapter, can be obtained by using the online estimator at www.socialsecurity.gov/estimator.

The PIA for each person is based on detailed calculations. For family retirement planning, it is important to understand a few key features of the calculations. This monthly benefit payment is a portion of the worker's **Average Indexed Monthly Earnings** (AIME) for the 35 years of highest earnings, where earnings for years before age 60 are indexed to reflect increases in U.S. workers' average wage level. For example, if the average wage level in the U.S. is twice as high when the individual is 60 than when he was 40, the formula doubles the age-40 earnings. If the worker has less than 35 years of income, the incomes are entered as zero for the remainder of the 35 years. The maximum income for any year is equal to that year's maximum income subject to Social Security taxes, which is $106,800 in 2011.

Stated another way, AIME is the average monthly earnings after indexing for the worker's highest earning 35 years. AIME is converted to Primary Insurance Amount. For someone born in 1948, PIA equals:

(90% of the first $761 of AIME) +
(32% of the next $3,825 of AIME) + (15% of additional AIME)

The amounts $761 and $4,586 ($761 + $3,825) are known as the **bend points**. Bend points are determined by the Social Security Administration and vary by year of birth.[4]. Therefore, for someone born in 1948, an AIME of $6,000 converts to a PIA of $2,121. This formula, with its decreasing percentages of 90%, 32% and 15%, ensures that Social Security benefits replace a higher percentage of earned income at lower income levels. Due to this 90%-32%-15% format, Social Security payments may replace 60% of pre-retirement income for someone earning minimum wage, but only 28% of income for someone earning the maximum income subject to Social Security taxes. For someone who earns twice the maximum income subject to Social Security taxes, Social Security benefits may replace only 14% of income.

4 Bend points are the dollar amounts of AIME where the percentages change from 90% to 32% and from 32% to 15%. These bend points vary by year of birth due to COLAs. They are so named because when PIA is graphed against AIME, the line bends at these points.

An understanding of the formulas is useful in decisions concerning how long to continue working. For instance, suppose Joe already has 35 years of earnings history when he reaches age 62. If he works four more years and then begins Social Security benefits, earnings from the next four years will likely replace four lower earning years. This substitution for lower wages will likely have little impact on his AIME. Moreover, since he is already in the 15% portion of the formula that converts AIME to PIA, his PIA would not be appreciably higher if he works four more years than it is today. However, a mother who returned to the workforce after raising children may be in the 90% or 32% portions of the formula that converts AIME to PIA, and thus be able to appreciably raise her PIA by working a few more years.

Are benefits adjusted based on work performed after benefits begin? Workers may receive increased benefits for work performed after beginning Social Security benefits. Each year, the Social Security Administration (SSA) reviews the records for all Social Security recipients who work. If the latest year of earnings turns out to be one of the highest 35 years, they recalculate the benefit and pay any increase due. This is an automatic process, and benefits can be paid as early as April of the next year for employees or as late as December for self-employed individuals. For example, between April 2011 and December 2011, increases will be paid for 2010 earnings if those earnings raised eligible benefits. The increase would be retroactive to January 2011.

Summary

In this chapter, we defined important Social Security terms. We explained the term Full Retirement Age, the reductions in benefits for beginning Social Security early, and the delayed retirement credits for postponing the start of benefits until after attaining FRA. We also explained the term Primary Insurance Amount. The PIA is a key input in the software tool since benefits are usually based on this amount.

Appendix 2A: Understanding *Your Retirement Benefits Estimate*

Until March 29, 2011, the Social Security Administration sent out an annual statement to individuals about three months before their birthday. Today, individuals can get the same information in *Your Retirement Benefit Estimate*, including an estimate of their Primary Insurance Amount, from the online estimator at www.socialsecurity.gov/estimator. You will be asked to input your name and other information meant to identify you. In addition, it will ask for your estimate of earned income in the last year.

To explain the information this *Estimate* conveys, let's look at a typical example. Joe inserted the requested information and received the following *Estimate*. It may say:

> *Assuming you continue to earn the same amount, if you*
>
> - *wait to start your benefits at your **full retirement age** (66 Years and 00 Month(s) for you), your monthly benefit will be about...$2,180.00.*
>
> - *delay starting your benefits until **age 70**, your monthly benefit will be about...$2,880.00.*
>
> - *stop working at **age 62** and start receiving Social Security benefits, your monthly benefit will be about...$1,623.00.*
>
> ***Assumptions:*** *We estimate your benefits using your average earnings over your working lifetime. If you worked last year, we will also assume that you will continue to work and make about the same amount as you entered for last year's earnings.*

These estimates do not include:

- *Medicare premiums or other amounts that may be deducted from your benefit.*

- *Any Social Security benefits you may be eligible for on the record of your current, divorced, or deceased former spouse.*

The *Estimate* presents the levels of projected monthly benefits in today's dollars if Joe were to begin benefits at age 62, at his Full Retirement Age (66 in this example), or at age 70. These projections assume he will continue to earn his current level of inflation-adjusted income (or, at least, the maximum annual income subject to Social Security taxes) until benefits begin. If Joe retires at age 62 and begins receiving benefits at age 62—which are two separate decisions—then he can expect an inflation-adjusted monthly income of $1,623 for the rest of his life. If he continues to work until Full Retirement Age (FRA) and then retires and begins receiving payments, he would get $2,180 a month. If he works until 70 and then begins receiving payments, the projected monthly income is $2,880. All benefit levels are stated in today's dollars. So, if cumulative inflation is 20% before benefits begin, the nominal payments will be 20% higher, but goods and services will also cost 20% more.

To repeat, the *Estimate* presents the levels of monthly benefits at various ages assuming Joe continues to work until the date that benefits begin. Suppose Joe plans to stop working at 62, and is deciding whether to begin benefits at 62, Full Retirement Age (66), or 70. The $1,623 benefit level would be a good estimate of his benefits if begun at age 62. If he stops working at 62 but begins benefits at 66, he would get approximately $2,164, [$1,623/0.75, where 0.75 reflects the 25% benefit reduction at age 62 from Table 2.1]. The $2,180 figure in the *Estimate* is slightly higher than $2,164, which reflects the increase in benefits from continuing to work from age 62 to 66. Similarly, if he stops working at 62 but begins benefits at 70, he would get approximately $2,856, [$2,164x1.32, where 1.32 reflects the 32% delayed retirement credit for beginning benefits at 70 from Table 2.1]. The $2,880 is slightly higher than $2,856, which reflects the increase in benefits from continuing to work from age 62 to 70. The projected level of $2,180 in benefits at FRA is a good estimate of the Primary Insurance Amount, and is an easy estimate to attain. Assuming he quits work at 62 but begins benefits at 66, a better estimate of his PIA may be the projected benefit level at 62 divided by (1 − benefit reduction fraction at 62), that is, $2,164 in this example.[5]

The *Estimate* provides no guidance about reductions in benefits for workers who will receive a pension from work not covered by Social Security. These reductions, which are usually substantial, are described in the Windfall Elimination Provision and Government Pension Offset. More information on estimating WEP's or GPO's effect on Social Security benefits can be found in Chapters 5, as well as at www.socialsecurity.gov/WEP or www.socialsecurity.gov/GPO.

---

[5] The goal of this book and the software tool is to help individuals make good decisions about when to begin Social Security benefits. Since future earnings are uncertain, the exact PIA may be unknown and must be estimated. In addition, the monthly benefit level is rounded down to the next lower dollar (unless it is already a whole dollar amount).

CHAPTER 3 Singles Strategies

We begin this chapter with a discussion of a key lesson. We present two criteria individuals should use when deciding when to begin Social Security benefits. Finally, we present an example that proves useful when helping clients understand the difference between the two criteria, and we discuss why most clients will want to consider both criteria when selecting their Social Security claiming strategy.

The singles strategies in this chapter assume that no one else can receive benefits based on this single individual's earnings record. If children or parents can receive benefits based on the single's earnings record, he or she should read Chapter 5. Also, this chapter and, indeed, this book are based on the benefits promised by the Social Security program at the time of publication.

Key Lesson

This section presents a key lesson that is useful for singles and couples who are deciding when to begin Social Security benefits.

Lesson 1	If a single individual lives to age 80, the cumulative lifetime benefits will be approximately the same whether benefits begin at 62, 63, 64, or any age through 70.

Although this chapter only discusses one lesson, the next chapter adds two more. Lesson 1 is not an accident. The Social Security Administration's actuaries set the reductions to benefits for beginning benefits before Full Retirement Age (FRA) and the delayed retirement credits for delaying benefits until after FRA so that they would be approximately actuarially fair.

Table 3.1 presents the cumulative lifetime benefits through ages 70, 75, 80, and so on in five year increments through age 100 if Social Security benefits begin at ages 62 through 70. It assumes the individual has a Full Retirement Age of 66 and Primary Insurance Amount of $2,000, but the relative sizes of cumulative lifetime benefits are identical for other PIA levels. All benefit amounts are expressed in today's inflation-adjusted dollars. Therefore, cumulative benefits represent the lifetime consumption power of Social Security benefits (ignoring taxes).

The age 80 column in Table 3.1 illustrates this lesson. If the single retiree lives to 80, cumulative lifetime benefits are similar no matter what age benefits begin. Furthermore, age 80 is the age where cumulative benefits are closest no matter when benefits actually begin.[6]

Table 3.1 also demonstrates that if a single individual has a much shorter-than-average lifetime, cumulative benefits are maximized when benefits begin at 62. And if the individual has a much longer-than-average lifetime, cumulative benefits are maximized when benefits begin at 70. For example, if the single individual lives to 75, cumulative lifetime benefits are maximized at $234,000 when benefits begin at 62. This cumulative benefits level is $18,000 larger than if benefits begin at 66 and more than $75,000 larger than if benefits begin at 70. If the individual lives to 95, cumulative lifetime benefits are maximized at $792,000 when benefits begin at 70. This cumulative benefits level is almost $100,000 larger than if benefits begin at 66 and almost $200,000 larger than if benefits begin at 62.

---

6 Closest is measured by minimum standard deviation of cumulative lifetime benefit levels when benefits begin at ages 62 through 70. This standard deviation is minimized when the lifetime is 80 (rounded to the nearest year).

Table 3.1.	Cumulative Lifetime Benefits through Ages 70 to 100 if Social Security Benefits Begin at Ages 62 through 70						
Ages	70	75	80	85	90	95	100
62	**$144,000**	**$234,000**	$324,000	$414,000	$504,000	$594,000	$684,000
63	$134,400	$230,400	$326,400	$422,400	$518,400	$614,400	$710,400
64	$124,800	$228,801	$332,801	$436,802	$540,802	$644,802	$748,803
65	$112,000	$223,999	$335,999	$447,998	$559,998	$671,998	$783,997
66	$96,000	$216,000	$336,000	$456,000	$576,000	$696,000	$816,000
67	$77,760	$207,360	**$336,960**	$466,560	$596,160	$725,760	$855,360
68	$55,680	$194,880	$334,080	$473,280	$612,480	$751,680	$890,880
69	$29,760	$178,560	$327,360	**$476,160**	$624,960	$773,760	$922,560
70	$0	$158,400	$316,800	$475,200	**$633,600**	**$792,000**	**$950,400**

Primary Insurance Amount is $2,000 with Full Retirement Age of 66. The bold number in each column indicates the highest cumulative lifetime benefit for that age.

Figure 3.1 illustrates the cumulative benefits by age for someone who lives to 100 if she begins benefits at ages 62, 66, and 70. If the individual lives to 80, cumulative benefits are approximately the same whether benefits begin at 62, 66, or 70. Is she dies well before age 80, her cumulative benefits are highest when she starts benefits at age 62. If she lives well beyond age 80, her cumulative benefits are maximized when she starts benefits at age 70. Whether the numbers in Table 3.1 or the graphs in Figure 3.1 are considered, it is clear that expected lifetime is one factor that should affect a single individual's starting date.

| Figure 3.1. | Cumulative Lifetime Benefits by Age if Benefits Start at 62, 66, and 70 |

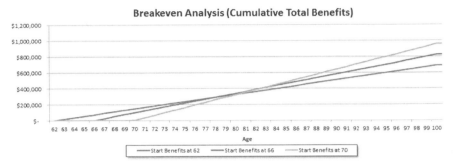

This graph shows cumulative lifetime benefits for a single individual with a Primary Insurance Amount of $2,000 if she begins benefits at ages 62, 66, and 70. She is assumed to live to age 100.

Two Criteria

Retirees should consider two criteria when deciding when to begin Social Security benefits.

> **Criterion 1:** Which starting date for singles or dates for couples will maximize expected cumulative lifetime benefits?

> **Criterion 2:** Which starting date for single or starting dates for couples will minimize **longevity risk**, that is, the risk that the single retiree will deplete her financial portfolio during her lifetime or the couple will deplete their portfolio during their joint lifetime?

Criterion 1, maximize expected cumulative lifetime benefits: As we saw in Table 3.1 and in Figure 3.1, if a single individual expects to die well before 80, she will maximize expected lifetime benefits by starting benefits at 62. If she expects to live well past 80, she will maximize expected lifetime benefits by delaying benefits until 70.

A closer look at the Social Security benefits formulas reveals subtle differences in breakeven ages between any two starting dates. Table 3.2 presents breakeven ages for starting Social Security benefits at age 62 instead of 63 (62 versus 63), 63 instead of 64, 64 instead of 65, and so on through starting benefits at 69 instead of 70. For example, the breakeven age of 78 means that the cumulative benefits are the same if a single individual starts benefits at 64 or 65 and dies in the month of his or her 78th birthday. Table 3.2 also shows the breakeven ages for starting Social Security at age 62 instead of 66 and other combinations. The breakeven ages tend to be a couple of years sooner than age 80 in the early years (e.g., 62 versus 63 and 62 versus 66) and a few years later than 80 in the later years (e.g., 69 versus 70 and 66 versus 70).

Table 3.2.	Breakeven Ages for Beginning Social Security Benefits
Beginning Dates	**Breakeven Ages**
62 versus 63	78
63 versus 64	76
64 versus 65	78
65 versus 66	80
66 versus 67	79.5
67 versus 68	81.5
68 versus 69	83.5
69 versus 70	85.5
62 versus 66	78
66 versus 70	82.5
62 versus 70	80.5

The "62 versus 63" of 78 means that the breakeven age for delaying beginning benefits from age 62 to 63 is age 78. Therefore, if the individual lives past 78 then cumulative lifetime benefits will be higher by delaying benefits from age 62 to 63. The table assumes a Full Retirement Age of 66.

Let's consider the implications for single individuals who are only concerned about maximizing expected cumulative lifetime benefits. Although not evident from Table 3.2, if a 62 year old expects to live to age 77 (i.e., die in the month of his 77th birthday), he maximizes cumulative benefits by starting benefits at age 64. The reductions in benefits for starting benefits before FRA are 5/9% per month for the first 36 months and 5/12% per month for each additional month benefits begin before age 63. Since 5/9% is larger than 5/12%, the benefit of delaying benefits one more month increases at age 63. This pattern encourages individuals to delay the start of benefits until at least 64 unless they are confident they will not live to at least 77.

Next, let's consider the implications for singles of delaying the start of benefits beyond Full Retirement Age. The breakeven age between starting benefits at age 66 and 67 is 79.5 years. This relatively low breakeven age reflects the 2/3% per month delayed retirement credits for delaying the start of benefits beyond FRA. Because this 2/3% is larger than the 5/9% reduction in benefits for starting benefits before FRA, the breakeven age between starting benefits at 66 and 67 is lower than the breakeven age between starting benefits at 65 and 66. Although not indicated in Table 3.2, if a 62 year old expects to live until 82.5 then she would maximize expected lifetime benefits by delaying benefits until age 68. However, if she is also concerned about longevity risk, she may rationally opt to delay benefits beyond age 68.

Recall that Criterion 1 says: If a single individual dies well before 80, she will maximize lifetime benefits by starting benefits at 62. If she lives well past 80, she will maximize lifetime benefits by starting benefits at 70. The prior two paragraphs explain why we used the two qualifiers "well before" and "well after" in this book. These two qualifiers allow us to state Criterion 1 succinctly. Nevertheless, financial advisors should be aware of the breakeven ages in Table 3.2. The breakeven ages are 80 or lower for delaying Social Security benefits one more year at ages 62, 63, 64, 65, and 66, but the breakeven ages are above 80 for delaying benefits one more year at ages 67, 68, and 69. Therefore, it is easier to justify delaying the start of benefits from age 62 to 67 than from age 67 to 70.

This study compares claiming strategies based on expected cumulative lifetime benefits because it is easily understood by clients. Appendix 3A at the end of this chapter explains that financial theory insists that the criterion should be to maximize the present value of benefits. However, at least today (late 2010), maximizing the present value of benefits is essentially the same as maximizing cumulative lifetime benefits. We prefer to state this criterion as maximization of cumulative lifetime benefits because it is easier for most people to understand, while being consistent with the present value principle.

Criterion 2, minimize longevity risk: Longevity risk is primarily a problem for those who live long lives. To minimize this risk one should maximize Social Security benefits at age 70 and beyond, and this can be accomplished by delaying the beginning of benefits until 70.

Many clients probably approach the Social Security claiming decision thinking the sole criterion is to select the starting date that maximizes expected cumulative lifetime benefits. It is important for financial advisors to help clients understand that their claiming strategy also affects their portfolio's longevity. Many retirees are at least as concerned about minimizing the risk that they will deplete their portfolio during their lifetime. The following example helps illustrate this point.

This example and graph illustrate that delaying the start of Social Security can extend a financial portfolio's longevity. Figure 3.2 shows the values of a single retiree's financial portfolio if she begins Social Security benefit at 62, 64, 66, 68 and 70. She begins retirement in 2009 with $700,000 in a 401(k) and she spends $41,700 after taxes in real terms each year. Her Primary Insurance Amount is $1,500. If she begins benefits at 62 then the portfolio lasts 30 years. By delaying the start of Social Security benefits until 64, 66, 68, or 70, she can extend the portfolio's longevity by, respectively, 1+, 2+, 4+, or 6+ years, where 1+ indicates that the portfolio provides full funding for one more year plus part of a second. Thus beginning benefits at 70 instead of 62 extended the portfolio's longevity by more than six years.

| Figure 3.2. | Household Assets |

Figure 3.2: Household Assets

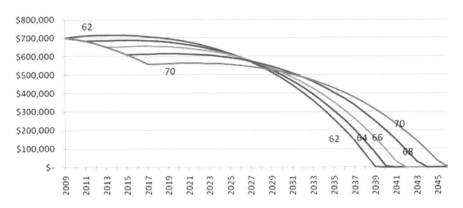

This example assumes the asset(s) earn 5% per year with inflation at 3% per year. It comes from a model developed at Retiree, Inc. The model assumes each year's taxes are based on then-current 2009 tax brackets, standard deduction amounts, personal exemption amounts, and deduction amount for being 65 or over all adjusted each year with inflation. It uses the three IRS formulas to calculate the taxable portion of Social Security benefits. See www.retieeinc.com for more information.

Reprinted with permission by the Financial Planning Association, Journal of Financial Planning, March 2010, William Meyer and William Reichenstein, "Social Security: When to Start Benefits and How to Minimize Longevity Risk." For more information on the Financial Planning Association, please visit www.fpanet.org or call 1-800-322-4237.

Figure 3.2 also does a good job of helping clients understand why both criteria may be important. If she has a much shorter-than-average lifetime, her beneficiaries will inherit the most if she begins benefits at 62. This is essentially the same statement as saying that if she has a much shorter-than-average lifetime, she will maximize cumulative lifetime benefits by starting benefits at age 62. If she has a much longer-than-average lifetime, she should begin benefits at 70. Not only will she maximize cumulative lifetime benefits, but her portfolio will last longer as well.

Consider two possibilities: she dies at a young age and she lives to an old age. If she dies at 75 at the beginning of 2022, her beneficiaries will inherit more if she begins benefits at 62 than at 70. But, as Figure 3.2 shows, they will still inherit a relatively large amount. If she lives until 95 and begins benefits at 62, her portfolio will be exhausted and she may be a financial burden on her children for her last three years. If she delays benefits until 70, her portfolio will last her lifetime and her beneficiaries will inherit a small amount. Some retirees are more concerned about not running out of money than about the amount of money their beneficiaries may inherit. These retirees are more concerned about longevity risk and should be especially interested in delaying benefits, possibly until age 70.

Figure 3.2 illustrates both criteria for this single retiree with moderate wealth. Therefore, we believe financial advisors can use it to help such clients understand the costs and benefits of delaying the start of Social Security benefits. The additional longevity from delaying benefits until 70 varies by level of wealth. Meyer and Reichenstein estimate that the additional longevity from delaying benefits from 62 to 70 is more than 12 years for singles with $500,000 in financial assets (all in a 401(k) or other tax-deferred account), while the additional longevity is more than three years for singles with $1 million in financial assets (all in a tax-deferred account).[7]

Conceptually, at lower levels of financial wealth, Social Security represents a larger portion of combined retirement resources, that is, financial assets plus Social Security. As discussed in Table 2.1, by delaying Social Security benefits from 62 to 70, the real benefit level increases by 76%. It should not be surprising, therefore, that delaying benefits can lengthen the longevity of a retiree's portfolio. Additional information can be found at www.SocialSecuritySolutions.com.

Recommended Strategies for Singles

As just discussed, there are two criteria that a single retiree should use when deciding when to begin Social Security benefits. The first criterion

7 See William Meyer and William Reichenstein, "Social Security: When to Start Benefits and How to Minimize Longevity Risk," *Journal of Financial Planning*, March 2010.

is to maximize expected cumulative lifetime benefits (or, the closely related, maximize the present value of lifetime benefits). The second is to minimize longevity risk. Each single individual's optimal claiming strategy depends on his or her expected lifetime and the relative importance of each criterion *to that specific person*. Obviously, a financial advisor cannot determine the relative importance of each criterion for a specific client. Nevertheless, he or she can make the following general statements. Singles who are relatively confident that they will die well before 80 will probably want to begin benefits as soon as possible. Singles who expect to live well past 80 will probably want to delay the start of benefits, probably until age 70. Singles who expect to live to about 80 and are concerned about longevity risk will probably want to delay benefits until after Full Retirement Age, possibly until as late as age 70.

To repeat, we cannot measure the relative importance of each criterion for a specific individual. However, most retirees are concerned with both criteria. We make the following general recommendations to singles in each of five groups with the accompanying wording. Each single individual falls into one and only one group. Obviously, if the single individual understands the two criteria, he or she can adjust our general recommendation as necessary to meet his or her specific preference.

Life expectancy of less than 75 years: This group consists of single individuals with expected lifetimes of less than 75 years. *We recommend beginning benefits as soon as possible—at age 62 or 62 and one month depending upon birth date—or as soon as all benefits would not be lost due to the earnings test. (The earnings test does not apply once an individual attains FRA.) We base this recommendation on your projected lifetime. If an individual dies before age 75, cumulative lifetime Social Security benefits will be highest if benefits are begun at age 62. However, be aware that, should the individual live to at least age 77, beginning benefits at 62 will result in lower lifetime benefits than starting benefits at age 64, and it could increase the risk that the financial portfolio will be exhausted during the individual's lifetime.*

Life expectancy of at least 75 but less than 77 years: This group consists of single individuals with expected lifetimes of at least 75 but less than 77 years. *We recommend beginning benefits at age 64. We base this recommendation on your projected lifetime. It is also important to consider two criteria when deciding when to begin benefits: maximizing expected cumulative lifetime benefits and minimizing longevity risk, that is, the risk of an individual depleting his financial portfolio in his lifetime. Assuming a Full Retirement Age of 66, if an individual dies at age 76 (the midpoint in this range), the cumulative lifetime benefits if benefits were begun at 64 will be 1% lower than if benefits were begun at 62. However, beginning benefits at 64 would also increase the monthly benefit by 15.6% and thus lower longevity risk should the individual live considerably longer than expected. We believe most single individuals in this group would consider starting benefits at 64 to be a good tradeoff between these two criteria.*

Life expectancy of at least 77 but less than 80 years: This group consists of single individuals with expected lifetimes of at least 77 but less than 80 years. *We recommend beginning benefits at age 67. We base this recommendation on your projected lifetime. It is also important to consider two criteria when deciding when to begin benefits: maximizing expected cumulative lifetime benefits and minimizing longevity risk, that is, the risk of depleting the financial portfolio in the individual's lifetime. Assuming a Full Retirement Age of 66, if an individual dies at age 78.5 (the midpoint in this range), cumulative lifetime benefits if benefits are begun at 67 will be about 1% less than the maximum cumulative benefit, which occurs if benefits are begun benefits at 64 years and nine months. However, beginning benefits at 67 instead of 64 years and nine months would increase the monthly benefit by 17.8% and thus lower the longevity risk should an individual live considerably longer than expected. We believe most single individuals in this group would consider starting benefits at 67 to be a good tradeoff between these two criteria.*

Life expectancy of at least 80 but less than 83 years: This group consists of single individuals with expected lifetimes of at least 80 but less than 83 years. *We recommend beginning benefits at age 69. We base this recommendation on your projected lifetime. It is also important to consider two criteria when deciding when to begin benefits: maximizing expected cumulative lifetime benefits and minimizing longevity risk, that is, the risk of depleting the financial portfolio in the individual's lifetime. Assuming a Full Retirement Age of 66, if an individual dies at age 81.5 (the midpoint in this range), cumulative lifetime benefits if benefits are begun at 69 will be about 1% less than the maximum cumulative benefit, which occurs if benefits are begun at 67 years and six months. However, beginning benefits at 69 instead of 67 years and six months would increase the monthly benefit by 10.7% and thus lower longevity risk should the individual live considerably longer than expected. We believe most single individuals in this group would consider starting benefits at 69 to be a good tradeoff between these two criteria.*

Life expectancy of at least 83 years: This group consists of single individuals with expected lifetimes of at least 83 years. *We recommend delaying the beginning of Social Security benefits until 70. We base this recommendation on your projected lifetime. It is also important to consider two criteria when deciding when to begin benefits: maximizing expected cumulative lifetime benefits and minimizing longevity risk, that is, the risk of depleting the financial portfolio in the individual's lifetime. Consider a single with a life expectancy of 83 years. Assuming a Full Retirement Age of 66, if an individual dies at 83 then cumulative lifetime benefits from starting benefits at 70 will be about 1% less than if she begins benefits at 69. However, beginning benefits at 70 instead of 69 would increase the monthly benefit by 6.5% and thus lower longevity risk should the individual live considerably longer than 83. We believe most single individuals in this group would consider starting benefits at 70 to be a good tradeoff between these two criteria. Individuals with life expectancies beyond age 83 should have an even stronger preference for delaying benefits until 70 since this starting date would likely maximize their expected cumulative benefits as well as minimize their longevity risk.*

Summary

In this chapter, we presented strategies for singles who are deciding when to begin Social Security benefits. We explained that there are two criteria that single individuals should use when deciding when to begin benefits. The first is to maximize cumulative lifetime benefits (or, the closely related, maximize the present value of lifetime benefits). The second is to minimize longevity risk, that is, the risk that the financial portfolio will be exhausted during the individual's lifetime. Lesson 1 is a key to the first criterion:

Lesson 1	If a single individual lives to age 80, the cumulative lifetime benefits will be approximately the same whether benefits begin at 62, 63, 64, or any age through 70.

Since longevity risk is primarily a problem for those who live long lives, to minimize this risk singles should maximize their benefits at age 70 and beyond by delaying the beginning of benefits until 70.

One goal of this chapter is to highlight that both criteria are important. Many clients probably approach the Social Security claiming decision thinking the sole criterion is to select the starting date that maximizes expected cumulative lifetime benefits. It is important for financial advisors to help clients understand that their claiming strategy also affects their portfolio's longevity. Once they understand this fact, they will be in a better position to rationally select the starting date that will best fit these dual criteria. Material in this chapter should help advisors convey this important point.

The bottom line: Each single individual should consider his or her life expectancy and the relative importance of the two criteria. Singles who are relatively confident they will die well before 80 will probably want to begin benefits as soon as possible. Singles who expect to live well past 80 will probably want to delay the start of benefits, probably until age 70.

Singles who expect to live to about 80 and are concerned about longevity risk will probably want to delay benefits until after Full Retirement Age, possibly until as late as age 70.

Finally, we presented in this chapter specific recommendations for each single person based on his or her life expectancy. These recommendations assume the retiree is concerned about both criteria. We believe the recommendation will fit most single individuals' tradeoff between the two criteria. Obviously, if the single individual understands the two criteria, he or she can adjust our general recommendation as necessary to meet his or her specific preference.

Appendix 3A: Maximizing Present Value of Benefits

Financial theory states that one criterion when deciding when to begin Social Security benefits should be maximization of the present value of benefits. This appendix explains that, at least in July 2010, this criterion is essentially the same as the criterion to maximize cumulative lifetime benefits because the after-tax real rate of return on Treasury Inflation Protection Securities (TIPS) is essentially zero. Even if this after-tax real rate of return rises, the maximization of present value is similar to maximization of cumulative lifetime benefits. We prefer to use the maximization of cumulative lifetime benefits to discuss the pros and cons of various claiming strategies because clients find it to be simple, understandable and intuitive. In contrast, it is hard to explain to clients the maximization of present value criterion. For example, if one claiming strategy provides cumulative benefits that are $80,000 larger than another claiming strategy then a client can understand that this $80,000 advantage is expressed in terms of today's purchasing power. In short and as explained here, the criterion to maximize cumulative lifetime benefits is consistent with the criterion to maximize the present value of benefits, but the former is easier to explain.

The two criteria—maximize cumulative lifetime benefits and maximize the present value of benefits—are essentially the same today.

Moreover, the two criteria will give similar recommendations even if after-tax real rates of return on Treasury securities rise a substantial 1%. Suppose inflation is 3% per year. Someone receiving $10,000 in Social Security benefits the first year will receive $10,300 the second year, $10,609 the third year, and so on. However, since prices are also rising by 3% a year, the $10,300 in the second year and $10,609 in the third year will buy the same amount of goods and services as $10,000 in the first year. If benefits are received for 22 years then cumulative lifetime benefits are $220,000 when all dollars are expressed in today's dollars.

Next, let's consider the present value criterion. The present value of $10,000 in Social Security benefits the first year, $10,300 the second year, $10,609 the third year, and so on for 22 years depends upon the after-tax rate of return that individuals can earn on similar-risk investments. If this after-tax rate of return is the inflation rate, then the present value of these payments for 22 years is $220,000, the same as cumulative lifetime benefits.

As of July 2011, the pretax real yield on 10-year TIPS is 0.5%. We used the 10-year yield because the duration of a 10-year TIPS bond is similar to the duration of a 20-year stream of Social Security benefits, and 20-years is a typical retiree's longevity. Assuming 2.5% inflation and 0.5% real return, TIPS investors will pay taxes on 3%. Assuming a 25% federal-plus-state marginal tax rate, the after-tax real return is essentially 0.0%. [Mathematically, it is slightly negative at -0.25% = 3%(1 − 0.25) − 2.5%, where 3%(1- 0.25) gives the after-tax return and 2.5% is the inflation rate]. Therefore, at least today, maximizing present value of benefits is essentially the same as maximizing cumulative lifetime benefits.

Since after-tax real rates of return vary, we discuss how other rates would change the breakeven period. At after-tax real (i.e., inflation adjusted) yields of 1%, 2%, and 3%, the present value of benefits are approximately equal if the single individual lives to, respectively, 81, 83, and 84.[8] So, if the after-tax real rates of return on TIPS should rise to 1% then the maximization of present value principle suggests that financial advisors

---

8 Mathematically, assuming a 1% annual discount rate, the standard deviation of cumulative lifetime benefits if benefits begin at ages 62 through 70 is lowest if the individual lives to age 81.

substitute 81 for 80 as the age when benefits would be approximately equal. We think this is a minor adjustment.

In short, although theory states that investors should be concerned with maximizing the present value of benefits, we prefer to state this criterion as maximizing cumulative lifetime benefits because it is easy for clients to understand while being consistent with the present value principle.

CHAPTER 4 Couples Strategies

Strategies for deciding the dates when each married partner should begin Social Security benefits often revolve around spousal benefits and survivor's benefits. Therefore, this chapter begins with descriptions of rules governing spousal benefits and survivor's benefits. We present two key lessons that apply specifically to couples strategies, as well as several couples examples designed to highlight ideas and insights related to couples' claiming decisions. Detailed examples for each of four couples groups will be provided, where each couples group is defined by the ratio of the spouses' low-to-high Primary Insurance Amounts. The claiming strategy that maximizes a couple's expected cumulative lifetime benefits depends upon the ratio of their PIAs. It also depends on their projected lifetimes, and at times, their relative ages. We will present recommended strategies for surviving spouses after the deaths of their partners, one of which will likely provide the maximum cumulative lifetime benefits.

Spousal And Survivor's Benefits

Claiming strategies for couples often revolve around spousal benefits and survivor's benefits. So we begin this chapter by describing rules governing these benefits. For clarity, we assume the wife receives spousal or survival benefits based on her husband's earnings record; however, the rules are parallel if the husband receives benefits based on his wife's earnings record.

Rules governing spousal benefits: Spousal benefits are benefits the wife receives based on the husband's earnings record when he is alive, while survivor's benefits are benefits the wife receives based on her husband's earnings record after he has died. Rules governing spousal benefits include the following:

1. Dual entitlement: She is entitled to the larger of benefits based on her earnings record or, if eligible, spousal benefits, which is up to 50% of her husband's Primary Insurance Amount.

2. Both spouses cannot receive spousal benefits at the same time.

3. In order for her to receive spousal benefits, her husband must have "filed for benefits based on his earnings record." For example, suppose she wants to file for spousal benefits based on his earnings record. For her to be eligible for spousal benefits, he must (1) already be receiving benefits based on his earnings record, or (2) once he reaches FRA, and she is eligible for spousal benefits, then she is deemed to be applying for both her own benefits and spousal benefits.

4. If she applies for benefits before attaining Full Retirement Age (FRA), and she is eligible for spousal benefits, then she is deemed to be applying for both her own benefits and spousal benefits. She will receive the larger of the two—her own benefits or spousal benefits (if eligible)—but not both. Stated differently, before attaining FRA she cannot apply for spousal benefits only and later switch to her own benefits, or vice versa.

5. After attaining FRA or later, she can apply for spousal benefits only, if eligible, and later switch to her own benefits, or vice versa.

6. If she has attained FRA (and her husband has filed), then she can make a restricted application for spousal benefits only and receive 50% of his PIA. Meanwhile, benefits based on her record would continue to accrue delayed retirement credits.

7. If she has not attained FRA (and her husband has filed), her spousal benefits are reduced by 25/36% for each of the first 36 months

and by 5/12% for each additional month that benefits are begun before she attains FRA.

The rules governing spousal benefits for a divorced spouse are slightly different as explained in Chapter 5.

An example covering six cases should help clarify spousal benefits. Suppose Jane is age 62 with a PIA of $800, and Jack is age 65 with a PIA of $2,000. Both have Full Retirement Ages of 66. Table 4.1 summarizes the cases.

- **Case 1:** *If he has already begun benefits* then she can apply for spousal benefits today. Since she is younger than FRA and eligible for spousal benefits, she is deemed to be applying for both her own retirement benefits and spousal benefits. At 62, benefits based on her earnings record is $600 a month, [75% x $800]. Her spousal benefit at 62 is $140 = 70% x ($1,000 - $800), where $1,000 is the **base spousal benefit** (that is, half his PIA), $800 is her PIA, so ($1,000 - $800) is her unreduced spousal benefit. She only receives 70% of this amount because she is applying for spousal benefits 48 months before attaining FRA. The reduction to 70% is calculated as 70% – 1 – 25/36% (36mos) – 5/12%(12mos) since she is starting spousal benefits 48 months before attaining Full Retirement Age. So, she receives $740 = $600 (own benefit at 62) + 0.7($1000-$800) (spousal benefit at 62).

- **Case 2:** He has not already begun benefits. One year hence at his FRA, he files and suspends benefits based on his earnings record. If she files at that time at 63, she is deemed to be applying for both her own benefits and spousal benefits because she is eligible for both. Benefits based on her earnings record is $640 a month, [80% x $800]. Spousal benefits at 63 = $150 = 75% x ($1,000 - $800). The ($1,000 - $800) is her unreduced spousal benefit but she only receives 75% of this amount because she is applying for spousal benefits 36 months before attaining FRA. So, her total benefit is $790 = $640 + $150.

- **Case 3:** She files today at 62. Since he has not filed for benefits, she is not yet eligible for spousal benefits. Today, she begins her own benefits of $600 a month as explained in Case 1. In one year, he files and suspends, which makes her eligible for spousal benefits. She files for spousal benefits at age 63 and receives $150 = 75% x ($1,000 - $800) in spousal benefits, where 75% is her spousal benefits fraction when applying 36 months before attaining FRA as explained in Case 2. Her total benefits at 63 are $750 = $600 (own benefits at 62) + $150 (spousal benefits at 63).

- **Case 4:** Like Case 3, she files today at 62. Since she is not yet eligible for spousal benefits, she begins retirement benefits based on her earnings record of $600 a month. In one year, he files and suspends, which makes her eligible for spousal benefits. However, unlike in Case 3, she defers spousal benefits until she turns FRA. At FRA, she begins spousal benefits and receives $800 = $600 her own benefits at 62 + ($1,000 - $800) additional spousal benefits, where $1,000-$800 is her unreduced spousal benefit at FRA, and she gets this full unreduced spousal benefit because she applied for it at FRA or later. In short, as in Case 3 she may add spousal benefits when he files and suspends his benefits, but as in Case 4 she may also delay adding spousal benefits until a later date, which would likely be at her FRA.

- **Case 5:** If she applies for benefits at FRA(66) (and he has filed), she will receive $800 retirement benefit based on her record + $200 spousal benefit, [$1,000 - $800], for a combined benefit of $1,000 a month. However, she should make a restricted application for spousal benefits only of $1,000 a month, half of his PIA. Then, when she turns 70, she can switch to benefits based on her earnings record of $1,056, [132% of $800], where 32% is her delayed retirement credits. Warning: If, at FRA, she does not restrict her application to a "spouse only" benefit, the Social Security agent will likely assume she is applying for her $800 retirement benefit + $200 spousal benefit. In this case, she would not be able to switch at 70 to $1,056 because she would not receive the delayed retirement credits since she began her own benefits at FRA.

- **Case 6:** If she applies for benefits at 67 (and he has filed), she will receive $864 retirement benefits based on her record, which reflects 12 months of delayed retirement credits, plus $136 in spousal benefits, [$1,000 - $864], for a combined benefit of $1,000 a month. As discussed in Case 5, at 67 she should restrict her application to a "spouse only" benefit of $1,000, half his PIA. Then, when she turns 70, she can switch to her retirement benefits of $1,056, [132% of $800].

In short, let's consider two situations. First, if she makes a restricted application for spousal benefits only after attaining FRA, then her spousal benefit will be the base spousal amount, half of his PIA. Second, she applies for her retirement benefits before FRA and applies for spousal benefits on or after the date she applies for her retirement benefits. In equation form, her retirement benefit = her PIA x reduced benefit factor, where the reduced benefit factor is less than 1 as explained in Table 2.1. In equation form, her spousal benefit = (base spousal benefit – her PIA) x spousal reduction factor, where the spousal reduction factor is less than 1 if she applies for spousal benefits before FRA and 1 if she applies at FRA. In such situations, both retirement benefits and spousal benefits are calculated separately, reduced separately when applicable with their own reduction factors, and then added together.

Table 4.1.	Jane's Retirement and Spousal Benefits in Six Cases					
Jane's age	**Case 1**	**Case 2**	**Case 3**	**Case 4**	**Case 5**	**Case 6**
62	$740		$600	$600		
63	740	$790	750	600		
64	740	790	750	600		
65	740	790	750	600		
66	740	790	750	800	$1,000	
67-69	740	790	750	800	1,000	$1,000
≥ 70	740	790	750	800	1,056	1,056

Jane is 62 with a Primary Insurance Amount of $800 and her husband is 65 with a PIA of $2,000. This table shows how her monthly benefits would vary depending upon when she begins benefits and, if not originally eligible for spousal benefits, when she applies for spousal benefits.

Rules governing survivor's benefits: For clarity, we present survivor's benefits as if the husband dies, but the rules are parallel if the wife dies. Survivor's benefits (also called **widow's or widower's benefits**) are benefits the wife receives based on her husband's earnings record after he has died. As explained in Chapter 2 and shown in Table 2.2, the Full Retirement Age for survivor's benefits can be different from the FRA for benefits based on her earnings record or spousal benefits. Rules governing survivor's benefits include the following:

1.   Dual entitlement: She is entitled to the larger of benefits based on her earnings record or survivor's benefits based on his record.

2.   She can receive full survivor's benefits when she attains FRA for widows or reduced benefits as early as age 60 (age 50 if disabled).

3.   Her survivor's benefits reflect his delayed retirement credits, if any.

4.   If she begins survivor's benefits after attaining her FRA for widows then she is entitled to the larger of (1) 82.5% of his PIA or (2) deceased spouse's monthly benefit amount, where the latter would include any delayed retirement credits if he began benefits after his FRA or he died after his FRA and had not started benefits based on his record.

5.   If she begins survivor's benefits before attaining her FRA for widows, her survivor's benefits will be reduced. If she begins benefits at 60, she will receive 71.5% of his full benefits. If she begins benefits at FRA for widows, she will receive 100% of his full benefits. The younger she starts benefits, the lower her monthly benefits will be with the reduction varying on a *pro rata* basis with her starting date between FRA for widows and age 60.

6.   This rule applies to situations where the deceased spouse did *not* begin benefits before his FRA but the widow begins survivor's benefits before attaining her FRA for widows. Her Full Widow's Benefit (defined below) will be reduced. Since he did not begin benefits before

his FRA, Full Widow's Benefit in this case is the larger of his PIA or his monthly benefit amount, where the latter includes any delayed retirement credits. If she begins benefits at 60 then she will receive 71.5% of Full Widow's Benefit. If she begins benefits at FRA for widows then she will receive 100% of Full Widow's Benefit. The younger she starts survivor's benefits the lower will be her monthly benefits with the reduction from Full Widow's Benefit varying on a pro rata basis with her starting date between FRA for widows and age 60.

7. Rule 7 applies to situations where the deceased spouse began benefits before his FRA and widow begins survivor's benefits before attaining her FRA for widows. In such cases, you need to calculate three amounts: (1) the deceased's retirement insurance benefit (Deceased's RIB), (2) 82.5% of the deceased's PIA and (3) the reduced widow insurance benefit (reduced WIB). Then these three numbers are aligned from low to high. Their sequence in Chart 1 determines which of these three amounts is her survivor's benefit.

In all cases except those where Rule 7 applies, the survivor's benefit in equation form is:

Survivor's benefits = survivor benefit fraction x Full Widow's Benefit,

where Full Widow's Benefit = Max(deceased spouse's monthly benefit amount, 82.5% of deceased spouse's PIA). For clarification, if his PIA is $2,000 and he began benefits three years early, then the deceased spouse's monthly benefit amount is $1,600. If he died two years before his FRA having never begun benefits, then his monthly benefit amount is $2,000. If he either began his benefits one year after his FRA or died one year after his FRA having never begun his retirement benefits then his monthly benefit amount is $2,160.

Several examples may help clarify survivor's benefits. In each example, his PIA is $2,000, her PIA is $800, and we assume FRA for all benefits is 66.

- **Case 1:** Her husband dies at 64 with a PIA of $2,000 having never begun his benefits. If she begins survivor's benefits when she is 60 (and she is not disabled), she will get $1,430 in benefits. If she begins survivor's benefits at 62, 64, or 66, then she will get $1,620, $1,810, and $2,000 a month with all dollars expressed in today's inflation-adjusted dollars. That is, the 28.5% reduction in the survivor benefit fraction at age 60 is prorated over the 72 month reduction period. In the equation, if her FRA for widow's benefits is 66, then the survivor benefit fraction is 0.715 if she is age 60, 0.81 at age 62 [$1,620/$2,000], 0.905 at 64, and 1 if she is FRA for widow's benefits or older. Full Widow's Benefit is $2,000. Note that Rule 7 does not apply because he did not begin benefits before his FRA.

- **Case 2:** His PIA was $2,000 and he dies at 67 having never begun benefits based on his earnings record. Full Widow's Benefit is $2,160, which is his PIA increased by 8% to reflect delayed retirement credits at the time of his death. If she begins survivor's benefits at FRA or later, then she gets $2,160. If she begins survivor's benefits before FRA, then her benefit amount is reduced as reflected in her survivor benefit fraction. In equation form, her survivor benefit fraction is 1 since she has attained FRA for widow's benefits.

- **Case 3:** His PIA was $2,000 and he dies at 69 having never begun benefits based on his earnings record. At his death, she is 60 and begins survivor's benefits immediately. She would get $1,773 a month (rounded down to whole dollar), that is, 71.5% of $2,480, where $2,480 reflects three years of delayed retirement credits on his benefits. In equation form, her survivor benefit fraction at age 60 is 0.715, while the Full Widow's Benefit is $2,480. If she delays the start of survivor's benefits until 63 or 66 (her FRA for widows), then she would be entitled to $2,126 or $2,480 a month.

- **Case 4:** His PIA was $2,000 and he dies at 64 having never begun his benefits. At his death, she is 60 and begins survivor's benefits immediately. She would get $1,430 a month, that is, 71.5% of $2,000, where 71.5% is survivor benefit fraction and $2,000 in the Full Widow's Benefit. If she waits until FRA for survivor's benefits, she would get $2,000 a month.

- **Case 5:** He began his benefits at his FRA at $2,000 a month. At his death, the Full Widow's Benefit is $2,000. Therefore, if she begins survivor's benefits at FRA or later, then she receives $2,000 a month.

- **Case 6:** His PIA was $2,000 but he began benefits based on his earnings at 62, so his monthly benefit level was $1,500. Later, he dies. She waits until FRA or later to begin survivor's benefits. Her survivor benefit fraction is 1. The Full Widow's Benefit is $1,650, that is, the larger of his monthly benefits, ⌈$1,500⌉, or 82.5% of his PIA, [$1,650]. She gets $1,650 in survivor's benefits. In essence, the 82.5%-of-his-PIA feature reduced the reduction in her survivor's benefits because her husband began his benefits early. For clarification, in this case she could have begun her own benefits before his death or after his death, but she cannot start her survivor's benefits until her FRA. That is, Rule 7 does not apply because she did not begin survivor's benefits before his FRA.

- **Case 7:** In this case, he began benefits based on his record before FRA and she begins survivor's benefits before her FRA. Thus Rule 7 applies. His PIA was $2,000, but he began benefits based on his earnings at 63, so his monthly benefit level was $1,600. He dies. She wants to begin widow's benefits at 60. She calculates three amounts: (1) the deceased number holder's retirement insurance benefit (Deceased's RIB), which is $1,600, (2) 82.5% of his PIA, which is $1,650, and (3) the reduced widow insurance benefit (reduced WIB), which is $1,430 (71.5% of his PIA, where 71.5% reflects the survivor benefit fraction at age 60). Then these three numbers are aligned from low to high. Since they follow Sequence 2 in Chart 1 below, her survivor's benefit is her reduced WIB of $1,430.

- **Case 8:** Repeat Case 7 except assume she wants to begin survivor's benefits at 64. Rule 7 applies. The three amounts are (1) $1,600 (Deceased's RIB), (2) $1,650 (82.5% of his PIA), and (3) $1,810 (reduced WIB, 90.5% of his $2,000, where 90.5% reflects the survivor benefit fraction at age 63). When aligned from low to high, they follow Sequence 6 in Chart 1. So, she gets $1,650 in survivor's benefits.

- **Terminology:** These Cases explain the rules that determine her total monthly survivor benefit amount. Using the Social Security Administration's terminology, it would separate this total into retirement and survivor's benefits. We ignore this separation in these Cases, so we could present the rules determining the total monthly benefits. For example, suppose her PIA is $800 and she begins benefits based on her own record at 63 of $640 a month. His PIA is $2,000 and he dies before FRA having never begun his benefits. As explained in Case 1, if she begins survivor's benefits at FRA or later, then she gets $2,000 a month. According to the SSA's terminology, her retirement benefit is $640 and her survivor's benefit is the remaining $1,340.

Chart 4.1 applies only to situations where Rule 7 applies. That is, it applies to cases where both the deceased spouse began benefits before FRA and the surviving widow begins survivor's benefits before FRA. It does not apply if the deceased spouse did not start benefits based on his record before FRA or the surviving spouse does not switch to survivor's benefits before FRA. For example, if the widow continues her own benefits until she attains FRA and then switches to survivor's benefits, then Chart 4.1 does not apply.

Chart 4.1.	The amount underlined in the sequence is the amount payable as survivor's benefit. Key: WIB – Widow Insurance Benefit, RIB – Retirement Insurance Benefit, DNH – Deceased Number Holder.		
	Low Amount	**Mid Amount**	**High Amount**
Sequence 1	**Reduced WIB**	82.5% Death PIA	DNH's RIB
Sequence 2	**Reduced WIB**	DNH's RIB	82.5% Death PIA
Sequence 3	82.5% Death PIA	**Reduced WIB**	DNH's RIB
Sequence 4	82.5% Death PIA	**DNH's RIB**	Reduced WIB
Sequence 5	DNH's RIB	**Reduced WIB**	82.5% Death PIA
Sequence 6	DNH's RIB	**82.5% Death PIA**	Reduced WIB

Key Lessons

Two key lessons apply specifically to couples strategies. In addition, we repeat Lesson 1 because it also helps explain when each partner should begin benefits. Remember, Lesson 1 stated that if a single individual lives to age 80, the cumulative lifetime benefits will be approximately the same no matter what age benefits begin. We will soon explain how this lesson applies to couples.

Lesson 2	The relevant life expectancy for the decision of when the spouse with the higher PIA should begin benefits based on his earnings record is the lifetime of the second spouse to die, while the relevant life expectancy for the decision as to when the spouse with the lower PIA should begin benefits based on her record is the lifetime of the first spouse to die.

Consider a married couple, Sam and Susan, both aged 62. Sam is the higher earning spouse and has a PIA of $2,000, while Susan has a PIA of $700. They both have FRAs of 66. Assume Sam will die at 75 and Susan will die at age 95, but the conclusion is the same if Susan dies at 75 and Sam dies at 95. How long will payments last for benefits based on Sam's, the higher earner's, record, and how long will payments last for benefits based on Susan's, the lower earner's, record?

Three of Sam's possible claiming strategies are to begin monthly benefits based on his record of $1,500 at age 62, $2,000 at 66, or $2,640 at 70. After Sam's death, Susan will receive survivor's benefits of $1,650, $2,000, or $2,640 a month *depending upon when Sam starts his benefits.* These benefits will continue until she dies at 95. So, benefits based on Sam's record will continue until the second spouse dies. If Sam begins benefits based on his record at 62, this couple will receive $1,500 a month from 62 until Sam's death at 75 and then $1,650 a month until 95. If he delays benefits until 66, this couple will receive $2,000 a month from age 66 to 95. If he delays benefits until 70, this couple will receive $2,640 a month from age

70 to 95. The relevant life expectancy for the higher earner is the lifetime of the second spouse to die.

Now, let's consider the claiming strategy for Susan, the lower earning spouse. Three of Susan's possible claiming strategies are to begin benefits on her record of $525 at 62, $700 at 66, or $924 at 70. But how long will these benefits last? The answer is that these benefits will last until the first spouse dies, in this case, until Sam dies at 75. If Susan begins benefits based on her record at 62, they will receive $525 from age 62 to 75. If she delays benefits until 66, they will receive $700 a month from age 66 to 75. If she delays benefits until 70, they will receive $924 a month from age 70 to 75. Benefits based on the lower earner's record will last until the first spouse dies. Thus, the relevant life expectancy for the decision as to when the lower earner should begin benefits is the lifetime of the first spouse to die. Several tables in this chapter will clearly illustrate this lesson.

Lesson 3	If at least one spouse lives well beyond the age that the higher earner turns 80, the couple's cumulative lifetime benefits will usually be highest if he delays benefits based on his record until age 70.

This is the most important lesson for most married couples. Consider Sam and Susan in the prior example. If Sam begins benefits based on his record at age 62, 66, or 70, the couple will receive $1,500, $2,000, or $2,640 per month in benefits, *and these payments will continue for as long as at least one partner lives.* If she lives to 90 and he dies sooner, this couple will receive $1,500 a month from 62 to 90, $2,000 a month from 66 to 90, or $2,640 a month from 70 to 90. This is essentially the same decision facing a single individual with a life expectancy of 90, which explains how Lesson 1 applies to couples. By delaying benefits based on his earnings record until 70, the couple will receive an inflation-adjusted 76% more per month than if he started these benefits at 62, and 32% more than if he started these benefits at 66. This also explains Lesson 3: If at least one partner lives well beyond the age that the higher earner turns 80, their cumulative lifetime benefits can be maximized if he delays benefits based on his record until age 70.

Now, let's change the example slightly. Suppose Susan, the lower-earning spouse, is 10 years younger than Sam. Sam has an even stronger incentive to delay benefits based on his earnings record until 70. By delaying until 70, Sam will ensure that Susan gets $2,640 each month for the rest of her life (instead of $2,000 if he starts benefits at 66 or $1,500 if he starts at 62). Since Susan will be 70 when Sam turns 80, there is an excellent chance that at least one partner will live well past the age that Sam, the higher earner, turns 80. Since Susan is so much younger, she probably will continue to receive this higher monthly benefit for many years after Sam's death.

Most couples will want the higher-earning spouse to delay benefits based on his record until age 70. The exception is when the couple is confident that both partners will die early, that is, well before the higher-earner turns 80. In this situation, neither spouse will live long enough to enjoy the higher level of benefits.

The reader should review the material in Chapter 3 that explains the meaning of the qualifier "well beyond" in Lesson 3. In particular, read the discussion under "Criterion 1, maximize expected cumulative lifetime benefits" and study Table 3.2. From Table 3.2 the breakeven ages between starting benefits at age 67 versus 68 is 81.5. The breakeven age between starting benefits at 68 versus 69 is 83.5, while the breakeven age between starting benefits at 69 versus 70 is 85.5. This helps explain the meaning of the qualifier "well beyond." It also explains that, if the second spouse is expected to die when the higher earner would be 83.5, they may want to have the higher earner start benefits at 69 instead of 70. This would slightly increase their expected cumulative lifetime benefits (compared to the strategy of him starting benefits at 70) if the surviving spouse lives to 83.5, but it would also increase the surviving spouse's longevity risk should he or she live significantly longer than expected. This is a tradeoff. But the general statement remains valid: If at least one spouse lives well beyond the age that the higher earner turns 80, the couple's cumulative lifetime benefits will be higher if he delays benefits based on his record until age 70.

Couples Examples

This section presents examples to illustrate that a couple's claiming strategy is important and to illustrate some of the lessons that determine when each partner should begin Social Security benefits.

Couple Example 1: Mike, age 62, has a PIA of $2,000. Frances, age 58, has a PIA of $1,600. They both have FRAs for all benefits of 66. Mike has a life expectancy of 80, and Frances has a life expectancy of 95. For simplicity, in all examples we assume the first month that benefits would be paid is January, so there are 12 monthly payments in the first year.

Table 4.2 summarizes two of their claiming strategies. In Strategy 1, they both begin benefits at 62. Mike receives $1,500 a month for the first four years. Then Frances turns 62 and receives $1,200 a month for a combined monthly benefit of $2,700. When he turns 80 and she is 76, Mike dies. After his death, Frances receives $1,650 a month until her death. As explained in Case 6 under "Rules governing survivor's benefits," her survivor's benefits would be $1,650. The Full Retirement Benefit is $1,650, that is, the larger of his monthly benefits, [$1,600], or 82.5% of his PIA, [$1,650]. Her survivor benefit fraction is 1 since she is FRA or older.

Table 4.2.		Couples Strategies, Example 1				
Frances/ Mike's Ages	Year	Strategy 1	Strategy 2	Difference (S2 - S1)	Wash	Gravy
58/62	1	$1500		-$1500	-$1500	
59/63	2	1500		-1500	-1500	
60/64	3	1500		-1500	-1500	
61/65	4	1500		-1500	-1500	
62/66	5	1200+1500	$1200+800	-700	-1500	$800
63/67	6	1200+1500	1200+800	-700	-1500	800
64/68	7	1200+1500	1200+800	-700	-1500	800
65/69	8	1200+1500	1200+800	-700	-1500	800
66/70	9	1200+1500	1200+2640	1140	1140	
67/71	10	1200+1500	1200+2640	1140	1140	
...	...	...	...	...	...	
75/79	18	1200+1500	1200+2640	1140	1140	
76/	19	1650	2640	990		990
77/	20	1650	2640	990		990
78/	21	1650	2640	990		990
...	...	...	...	...		...
94/	37	1650	2640	990		990
Cum Life-time Benefits		$901,800	$1,158,720	$257,040	-$7,200	$264,240

Frances is 58 with a Primary Insurance Amount of $1,600 and Mike is 62 with a PIA of $2,000. He dies at age 80 (i.e., in the month of his 80th birthday) and she dies at 95. The Difference column reflects monthly benefits in Strategy 2 less monthly benefits in Strategy 1.

In Strategy 2, Frances begins benefits in four years when she turns 62 and receives $1,200 a month. Mike begins spousal benefits only at that time and receives $800 a month, half of her PIA. (Since he has attained

FRA, he can file for spousal benefits only and later switch to benefits based on his earnings record.) When he turns 70, he switches to benefits based on his earnings record and receives $2,640 a month for combined monthly benefits of $3,840. Notice that the $2,640 reflects his delayed retirement credits since he had never begun benefits based on his earnings record. After his death, she retains his $2,640 monthly benefits.

The Difference (S2 - S1) column shows the difference in monthly benefits between Strategies 2 and 1. The columns labeled Wash and Gravy separate this Difference column into two components. The Wash column shows the difference between Mike's benefits if he were single, lived until age 80, and began benefits at 70 instead of 62.

Recall from Lesson 1 that if a single individual lives to age 80, the cumulative lifetime benefits will be approximately the same no matter what age benefits begin. The Wash column reflects this lesson. By delaying his own benefits from 62 until 70, he loses $1,500 a month for eight years but gets an extra $1,140 a month for 10 years, and these amounts are approximately offsetting. Therefore, the column labeled Gravy represents the approximate additional cumulative lifetime benefits from Strategy 2 compared to Strategy 1. In terms of cumulative benefits, these Gravy components are like free goods.

The Gravy column contains two components. The first is Mike's $800 a month in spousal benefits from his FRA through age 69. Munnell, Golub-Sass, and Karamcheva named this the **claim-now-and-more-later advantage**.[9] By delaying benefits based on his earnings record from age 62 until 70, he gets the additional $1,140 a month. From Lesson 1, $1,500 a month from age 62 until he turns 80 is comparable to $2,640 a month from age 70 until 80. However, he also gets the $800 a month in spousal benefits, which is like a free good.

The second component of the Gravy column is the additional $990 a month beginning when Mike dies and continuing until the second

9 See Alicia H. Munnell, Alex Golub-Sass and Nadia Karamcheva. 2009. "Strange but True: Claim Social Security Now, Claim More Later," Center for Retirement Research, April, no. 9-9.

partner dies, in this case Frances, when she turns 95. When Mike dies at 80, Frances is only 76, so this additional benefit lasts 19 years. We named this the **joint-lives advantage**.[10] Notice that the time horizon of this joint-lives advantage is from the death of the first spouse until the death of the second spouse. If one spouse dies early and the other dies late, this advantage will be especially large. Furthermore, if Frances were much younger than Mike, say 10 years younger, then this advantage would tend to be especially large.

Finally, although we assumed that Mike dies when he turns 80 and Frances dies 19 years later, the payments in Strategy 2 would be the same if Frances dies when Mike turns 80 and Mike dies 19 years later. After the death of the first spouse (and it does not matter who dies first), the survivor gets the $2,640 monthly benefit which lasts until the second spouse dies.

Example 1 illustrates that the relevant life expectancy for the benefits of the spouse with the higher PIA is the lifetime of the second partner to die. In both Strategies, his higher monthly benefit payment continues until the death of the second spouse. From Lesson 3, *as long as at least one spouse lives well beyond the age when the higher earner turns 80, the higher earner should delay benefits based on his record until 70.* From Table 3.2, the exact breakeven age for cumulative lifetime benefits varies, but it is close to age 80. The "well-beyond" qualification in the italicized sentence reflects the fact that the breakeven age may be slightly higher than 80. The next example further illustrates the principle that the relevant life expectancy for the higher earner is the lifetime of the last partner to die.

Couple Example 2: This example repeats Example 1, except it assumes Mike is 69 with terminal cancer and will die in one year, while Frances is 65, comes from long-lived ancestors and expects to live until 95. It may seem that Mike should begin benefits today. After all, he only has one year to live. But he should not. Let's compare two strategies. In Strategy 1, he begins benefits today at $2,480 a month, which reflects the 24% of

---

10 See William Meyer and William Reichenstein, "Social Security: When to Start Benefits and How to Minimize Longevity Risk," *Journal of Financial Planning*, March 2010.

delayed retirement credits, and this payment continues until Frances dies in 30 years. In Strategy 2, he does not begin benefits today. In one year, he dies and she begins survivor's benefits of $2,640 a month for 29 years. In Strategy 2, she gets $2,640 a month for 29 years, while in Strategy 1 she gets $2,480 a month for 30 years. Strategy 2 provides $25,920 more in cumulative lifetime benefits. This example clearly illustrates that it is the life expectancy of the second spouse to die that should affect the higher earner's claiming strategy.

Couple Example 3: Let's compare Mike's Social Security benefits in Strategy 2 of Example 1 with his benefits if Frances waits until 66 to file for her benefits. Recall that Mike would not be eligible for spousal benefits until Frances files for benefits. If Frances files for benefits at 66, Mike will be 70. Since he begins benefits based on his earnings record at 70, this means he would not get spousal benefits. Compared to his benefits in Strategy 2, he would lose $800 a month in spousal benefits for the four years from when he is 66 through 69. She would begin benefits of $1,600 a month at age 66 instead of $1,200 a month at age 62. However, this $1,600 would only last until the death of the first spouse, which is expected to be when Mike turns 80 and Frances turns 76. This example shows there are two reasons that she should begin her benefits at 62 instead of waiting until her FRA. First, if she begins her benefits at 62, Mike will be eligible to file for spousal benefits only at his FRA, so he will get the $800 a month for the 48 months from his FRA until he turns 70. Therefore, *when one spouse begins benefits can affect the other spouse's benefits, and it can be a factor determining the couple's best claiming strategy.* Second, she should start benefits at 62 because these benefits will only last until the death of the first spouse, when he would turn 80 and she turns 76. From Lesson 1, the cumulative benefits of her $1,200 monthly benefit from age 62 until 76 are larger than the cumulative benefits of $1,600 a month from age 66 until 76.

Couple Example 4: Let's continue with Example 1 except change their relative ages. In Example 4, assume Mike is 62 but Frances is 61, one year younger. As before, Mike has a PIA of $2,000 and Frances has a PIA of $1,600. He expects to die at 80 and her at 95. When should each partner begin benefits?

Let's address his claiming strategy first. Since at least one spouse will live well past the date the higher earner turns 80, he should delay the start of his benefits until 70. When should she begin benefits? In order for Mike to get spousal benefits when he turns FRA, she must have filed for benefits. So, she must file for benefits by 65. If she waits until 66 to apply for benefits, he will only receive three years of spousal benefits—the years when he is 67 through 69. Assuming he dies at 80 when she turns 79, Lesson 1 tells us that her benefits would be roughly similar whether she starts benefits at 62, 65, or any month in between.[11] However, she should start her benefits by 65 so he can get spousal benefits when he attains FRA. This example illustrates that the best decision for the lower-earning spouse sometimes revolves around what she must do to ensure that the higher earner can get spousal benefits. Therefore, the difference in their ages should sometimes influence her claiming strategy. The next three examples illustrate this point.

Couple Example 5: Repeat Example 1 except assume Mike is 62 and Frances is 56, six years younger. He expects to die at 80 and her at 95. When should each partner begin benefits?

In this case, he should delay benefits based on his earnings record until 70 so his much younger wife will get the $2,640 monthly benefit for the rest of her life. She should begin her benefits at 62, the earliest date possible, so he can get spousal benefits for as long as possible. When she is 62, he will be 68. So, if she applies for benefits at 62 he will be eligible for spousal benefits for two years, the years that he is 68 and 69. In addition, her benefits will only last until Mike dies when she will be 74. From Lesson 1, $1,200 a month from age 62 to 74 exceeds the cumulative benefits from starting at a later age.

---

11 From Table 3.2, projected benefits through age 79 are slightly higher if she begins benefits at 65 than 62 or 63 or 64. However, cumulative benefits are similar at all ages.

Couple Example 6: Repeat the same example except assume Frances is 54, eight years younger than Mike. He expects to die at 80 and she at 95. In this example, the higher earner will not be eligible for any spousal benefits. When the lower earner turns 62, the higher earner will already be 70 at which time he will have begun benefits based on his earnings record.

When should each partner begin benefits? Since Frances is expected to live well beyond the age that Mike would turn 80, he should delay his benefits until age 70 to ensure that his much younger spouse receives the $2,640 a month in survivor's benefits for the rest of her life. She should start her benefits at 62. Her benefits will only last until the first partner dies. If he dies when she reaches her 72nd birthday, her benefits would last 10 years. Since the lower-earner's benefit will only last until the first partner dies, if the lower earner is much younger, she will probably want to begin her benefits at 62.

Couple Example 7: Mike is 62 with a PIA of $2,000. Frances is 65, three years older than Mike, with a PIA of $1,600. They both have FRAs for all benefits of 66. Mike expects to die at 80 and she at 95. When should each partner begin benefits?

Since Frances is expected to live well beyond the age that Mike turns 80, he should delay his benefits until age 70. When should Frances begin benefits? Her benefits will last until the first partner dies when she is expected to be 83. So that Mike can receive four years of spousal benefits beginning when he turns FRA, Frances should either begin her benefits or file and suspend her benefits by age 69. Let's calculate expected cumulative benefits from her earnings record for two claiming strategies. First, she begins benefits at 69. In this case, she would receive $1,984 a month beginning at age 69 and lasting for 14 years for cumulative benefits from her record of $333,312, [$1,600 x 1.24 x 14 years x 12 months, where 1.24 reflects delayed retirement credits of 24%]. Second, she files and suspends her benefits by age 69 so Mike can receive four years of spousal benefits. At 70, she begins benefits based on her earnings record of $2,112, which reflects 32% in delayed retirement credits. In this case, she would receive $2,112 a month for 13 years for a total of $329,472. The expected cumulative benefits from her record would be similar in these two strategies. However, by delaying her benefits until she turns 70, they would maximize their combined monthly benefits after he turns 70 until the first partner dies. Therefore, if she delays her benefits until 70, they would minimize their longevity risk if both spouses should live long lives. The choice between these two claiming strategies depends on the relative importance to this couple of maximizing expected cumulative benefits and minimizing longevity risk if both partners live long lives.

Couple Example 8: This example repeats Example 1, except it assumes Frances plans to work from age 62 to 66. Mike is 62 with a PIA of $2,000. Frances is 58 with a PIA of $1,600. If she files for benefits at 62 then both her benefits and Mike's spousal benefits are subject to the earnings test, because both sets of benefits are based on her earnings record. From Strategy 2 in Table 4.2, if not for the earnings test their combined monthly benefits would be $2,000 a month when she is 62. As explained in Chapter 5, the earnings test will reduce these benefits by $1 for each $2 of earnings above $14,160 (in 2011). If Frances' earnings are sufficiently high then they would eliminate both her benefits and Mike's spousal benefits. Once she attains FRA then the earnings test would no longer apply. But suppose her earnings would reduce but not eliminate their $2,000 a month in joint benefits. In this case, they will maximize their expected cumulative lifetime benefits if she files for benefits at 62. Because Mike is expected to die before Frances turns 80, their cumulative lifetime benefits are expected to be higher with this strategy than for her to wait until attaining FRA to file for benefits. Details of the earnings test are discussed in Chapter 5. But the point to be made here is that it can pay for Frances to file for benefits at age 62 even though the couple would lose some of their $2,000 a month in joint benefits due to the earnings test.

Recommended Strategies for Four Couples Groups

For two years our firm has been engaged in Social Security research with the goal of creating a set of heuristics that would serve as a framework for crafting smart claiming strategies. The work is complicated and proprietary, but the result is a series of unique "buckets." Each couple falls into one bucket, where a bucket includes all couples that meet certain conditions. These conditions are based on the ratio of the spouses' low-to-high PIAs, the expected lifetime of each spouse, and their relative ages. We recommend one smart strategy for couples in each bucket. This initial strategy is a good strategy. However, the best strategy for a specific couple will depend in part on the tradeoff *for this couple* between the criteria of maximizing their expected cumulative lifetime benefits and minimizing their longevity risk. So, it is impossible for us or anyone else to define ahead of time the "best" strategy for a specific couple. Sometimes there is a strategy besides the recommended strategy that the couple will consider better. Occasionally, there is another strategy that rates as least as high by both criteria. After reading the discussion in this section and with practice, financial advisors will become better at figuring out how to come up with another strategy that might better fit the specific client's preferences. For example, if a client is more concerned with minimizing longevity risk than maximizing expected cumulative benefits then the advisor should pay particular attention on the size of monthly benefits received after both partners turn 70. This will help the advisor recommend another strategy that may better fit this client's unique risk-return preference.

In this section, we distinguish four couples groups that we call High Ratio, Medium Ratio, Medium Low Ratio, and Low Ratio. The four groups are defined relative to the ratios of their low-to-high PIAs, which is calculated by dividing the lower PIA by the higher PIA. Table 4.3 presents the ranges of PIA ratio for each group.

Table 4.3.	Range of Ratio of Low-to-High PIAs for Couples Groups	
Group	**PIA Ratio Range**
High Ratio	≥ 0.5
Medium Ratio*	0.379 to 0.499
Medium Low Ratio*	0.334 to 0.378
Low Ratio	≤ 0.333

Assumes FRA of 66 for younger spouse.

For each group, we present a detailed example covering several claiming strategies. For each group, we also present a table that shows the sizes of the strategies' cumulative lifetime benefits for various combinations of each partner's life expectancy. Based on the discussion in each section, an advisor should be able to recommend one or a few smart claiming strategies. In addition, the advisor should be able to explain the relative advantages and disadvantages of each of these smart strategies. With this information, the client will be in a position to make an informed decision as to which claiming strategy best fits their risk-return preference.

Please note that several strategies call for at least one partner to begin Social Security benefits as soon as possible. As discussed in Chapter 5 (see Date Issues), some people are first eligible for benefits in the month they attain age 62, but most people must wait until the month they attain 62 years and one month. For simplicity, we assume benefits can begin at age 62. However, even if a partner must wait until age 62 years and one month to begin benefits, it should not affect the relative appeal of the strategies.

Couple Example 8, High Ratio couple: The High Ratio group consists of couples with a ratio of low-to-high PIAs that is greater than or equal to 0.5. The only way for either partner in a High Ratio couple to benefit from spousal benefits is if he or she begins spousal benefits only at FRA or later and then switches at a later date to benefits based on his or her own earnings record.

Table 4.4 presents the monthly Social Security benefits for a High Ratio couple given various strategies assuming the wife dies at 95 and the husband dies at 74. For clarity, when we say someone dies at 74, we mean he or she dies in the month of his or her 74th birthday. Wilma is 59 with a PIA of $1,600. Henry is 62 with a PIA of $2,000. They are a High Ratio couple because $1,600/$2,000 is greater than or equal to 0.5. They both have FRAs for all benefits of 66. As before, we assume benefits begin in January, but the relative appeal of the strategies is not affected by this assumption.

Table 4.4.	Combined Monthly Benefits from Six Strategies for a High Ratio Couple				
Wilma/ Henry's Ages	Strategy 1	Strategy 2	Strategy 3	Strategy 4	Strategy 62
59/62				$1500	$1500
60/63				1500	1500
61/64				1500	1500
62/65	$1200			1500	1200+1500
63/66	1200+800	$1280+800		1500	1200+1500
64/67	1200+800	1280+800		1500	1200+1500
65/68	1200+800	1280+800		1500	1200+1500
66/69	1200+800	1280+800	$1,000	1000+1500	1200+1500
67/70	1200+2640	1280+2640	1000+2640	1000+1500	1200+1500
68/71	1200+2640	1280+2640	1000+2640	1000+1500	1200+1500
69/72	1200+2640	1280+2640	1000+2640	1000+1500	1200+1500
70/73	1200+2640	1280+2640	2112+2640	2112+1500	1200+1500
71/	2640	2640	2640	2,112	1650
72/	2640	2640	2640	2112	1650
...	...	...	...		...
92/	2640	2640	2640	2112	1650
94/	2640	2640	2640	2112	1650
Cum Lifetime Benefits	$1,055,040	$1,048,320	$960,384	$757,344	$820,800

Wilma is 59 with Primary Insurance Amount of $1,600 and Henry is 62 with PIA of $2,000. He dies at age 74 (i.e., in the month of his 74th birthday) and she dies at 95.

In Strategy 1, Wilma begins benefits at 62 and receives $1,200 a month. One year later when he attains FRA, Henry begins spousal benefits of $800 a month for a combined monthly benefit of $2,000. At 70, he switches to benefits based on his earnings record of $2,640 a month. After his death, she gets $2,640 a month in survivor's benefits for the rest of her life.

In Strategy 2, Wilma begins benefits at 63 because that is when Henry turns FRA. Recall that Wilma must file for her benefits for Henry to be eligible for spousal benefits. In order for him to get four full years of spousal benefits, she must file for benefits no later than the month that he turns FRA. When she is 63, she gets $1,280 a month based on her earnings record, while he files for spousal benefits only of $800 a month for combined monthly benefits of $2,080. At 70, Henry switches to benefits based on his earnings record and receives $2,640. After his death, Wilma gets $2,640 a month in survivor's benefits for the rest of her life.

In Strategy 3, Henry files and suspends his benefits sometime between the month he attains FRA and the month Wilma attains FRA. This makes her eligible to apply for spousal benefits only when she attains FRA. She files for spousal benefits of $1,000 a month at FRA. One year later, Henry turns 70 and begins benefits based on his earnings record of $2,640 a month for combined monthly benefits of $3,640. When Wilma turns 70, she switches to benefits based on her earnings record of $2,112 for a combined monthly benefit of $4,752. After Henry's death, she gets $2,640 a month in survivor's benefits for the rest of her life.

In Strategy 4, Henry applies for benefits at age 62 and receives $1,500 a month. Wilma begins spousal benefits only when she attains FRA and receives $1,000. At 70, she switches to benefits based on her earnings record and receives $2,112 a month. After Henry's death, she gets $2,112 a month.

In Strategy 62, they both begin benefits at 62. Henry receives $1,500 this year. At 62, Wilma begins her benefits of $1,200 for a combined monthly income of $2,700. After his death, she gets $1,650 a month for the rest of her life as explained in Case 6 under "Rules governing survivor's benefits."

Table 4.5 presents this couple's cumulative lifetime benefits for various combinations of dates of death for each partner. The first row shows their cumulative benefits that correspond to Table 4.4, where Wilma dies at 95 and Henry dies at 74; in our notation, this is W95/H74. In this case, they maximize their cumulative lifetime benefits with Strategy 1. Let's examine when each partner should begin benefits to maximize their cumulative lifetime benefits.

Table 4.5.	Cumulative Lifetime Benefits for a High Ratio Couple				
Ages of Death	Strategy 1	Strategy 2	Strategy 3	Strategy 4	Strategy 62
W95/H74	**$1,055,040**	$1,048,320	$960,384	$757,344	$820,800
W95/H83	1,184,640	1,186,560	**1,188,480**	985,440	934,200
W95/H93	1,328,640	1,340,160	**1,441,920**	1,238,880	1,060,200
W85/H83	867,840	869,760	**871,680**	805,440	736,200
W75/H83	**637,440**	634,560	586,560	625,440	565,200
W95/H66	782,400	768,000	801,600	**824,450**	720,000
W73/H73	343,680	336,000	238,080	358,032	**372,600**

W95/H74 indicates that Wilma dies at 95 and Henry dies at 74. Bold denotes the largest cumulative lifetime benefits.

Henry, the higher earner, should delay benefits based on his record until age 70 because at least one partner lives well past the time that he would reach 80. In Strategies 1 through 3, where Henry defers benefits based on his record until 70, the couple's cumulative lifetime benefits are about $140,000 to $234,000 larger than when he begins benefits at age 62 in Strategy 62. When should Wilma, the lower earner, begin benefits to maximize their lifetime benefits? Since the first spouse dies before she turns 80, she should begin benefits as early as possible. Thus, Strategies 1 and 2 provide more benefits than Strategy 3.

The second row shows their cumulative benefits if Wilma dies at 95 and

Henry dies at 83. This combination was chosen because she will be 80 when he turns 83. The lower earner's benefits last until the first spouse dies (in this case, when she is 80), and from Lesson 1 we know her cumulative benefits are similar no matter when benefits begin. Therefore, the cumulative benefits for Strategies 1 through 3 are similar. In this example, Strategy 3 provides more lifetime benefits than Strategies 1 and 2. In other cases, Strategy 1 or 2 will provide more lifetime benefits than Strategy 3. You must run the numbers each way to determine which strategy provides the largest lifetime benefits. Remember, however, that most retirees are also concerned about longevity risk. Strategy 3 provides the highest combined monthly benefits after age 70 and thus minimizes their longevity risk should both partners live long lives.

The third row of the table (labeled W95/H93), shows the cumulative benefits if they both live a long time. In this case, Strategy 3 provides the largest lifetime benefits, and its advantage compared to Strategy 1 or 2 exceeds $101,000. Since the lower earner delays benefits based on her record until 70, they enjoy the $4,752 combined monthly benefits for a long time. If both partners live beyond the date that the lower earner turns 80, Strategy 3 usually provides the largest cumulative lifetime benefits.

Comparisons of W95/H83, W85/H83, and W75/H83 show how her longevity will affect their preferred strategy, holding his longevity constant. In W75/H83, she dies early. So, Strategies 1 and 2 have large advantages compared to Strategy 3 when benefits start relatively late in life. In W85/H83 and W95/H83, the first spouse dies when the lower earner turns 80. So, Strategies 1 through 3 provide similar lifetime benefits.

For W95/H66, Strategy 4 provides the highest cumulative benefits. This strategy may be best if the higher earner dies at or before attaining FRA, especially if the two PIAs are similar. The key to understanding why and when Strategy 4 is best is to compare the lower-earner's benefits at 70 based on her earnings record and the benefit level the higher earner would have been eligible for if he applied for benefits at his death. In this example, her benefits at 70 of $2,112 a month exceed the $2,000 a month he would have been eligible for had he begun benefits at his death at age 66. Strategy 4 applies to situations such as this. At his death, she should take his survivor's benefits and then switch to her benefits of $2,112 a month when she turns 70. The benefit totals for W95/H66 reflect survivorship rules. Recommended strategies for surviving spouses are discussed later in this chapter.

Finally, the H73/W73 row indicates that, if both partners die very early, it pays for both partners to begin benefits as soon as possible. However, even in this case, Strategy 62 only has about a $14,500 cumulative lifetime advantage compared to Strategy 4 and about a $29,000 advantage compared to Strategy 1. Unless they are confident that both partners will die early, they may prefer the reduction in longevity risk offered by Strategies 1 and 4 instead of Strategy 62. In short, High Ratio couples where both partners have short life expectancies should consider Strategies 1, 4, and 62 and consider the possibility that at least one partner lives longer than he or she expects.

In most cases, when at least one partner lives past the age when the higher earner turns 80, Strategies 1, 2, or 3 will maximize a High Ratio couple's cumulative lifetime benefits. The relative attractiveness of these strategies depends in part upon the partners' relative ages because their relative ages affect the number of years each partner is eligible for spousal benefits. All three strategies should be evaluated. In general, couples where the higher earner is four or more years older than the lower earner will tend to prefer Strategy 3. Couples where the higher earner is younger than the lower earner will tend to prefer Strategy 1 or 2.

Couple Example 9, Medium Ratio couple: This section presents recommended strategies for couples with a ratio of low-to-high PIAs that is greater than or equal to 0.379 but less than 0.5 assuming the younger spouse has a FRA of 66.

Table 4.6 presents the monthly Social Security benefits for Luke and Sara, a Medium Ratio couple, for various claiming strategies assuming he dies at 83 and she dies at 95. Luke is 62 with a PIA of $2,200 and Sara is 61 with a PIA is $1,000. They both have FRAs of 66. They are a Medium Ratio couple because $1,000/$2,200 is 0.45, which is greater than or equal to 0.379 but less than 0.5.

Table 4.6.	Combined Monthly Benefits from Five Strategies for a Medium Ratio Couple				
Sara/ Luke's Ages	Strategy 1	Strategy 2	Strategy 3	Strategy 4	Strategy 62
61/62					$1650
62/63	$750				820+1650
63/64	750				820+1650
64/65	750				820+1650
65/66	750+500	$933+500			820+1650
66/67	750+500	933+500	$1100	$1000+500	820+1650
67/68	750+500	933+500	1100	1000+500	820+1650
68/69	750+500	933+500	1100	1000+500	820+1650
69/70	850+2904	1033+2904	1100+2904	1100+2904	820+1650
70/71	850+2904	1033+2904	1320+2904	1100+2904	820+1650
...	...	...	...	...	...
81/82	850+2904	1033+2904	1320+2904	1100+2904	820+1650
82/	2904	2904	2904	2904	1815
83/	2904	2904	2904	2904	1815
...	...	...	...	...	...
94/	2904	2904	2904	2904	1815
Cum Lifetime Benefits	$1,125,648	$1,135,980	$1,148,928	$1,131,648	$895,740

Sara is 61 with a Primary Insurance Amount of $1,000 and Luke is 62 with a PIA of $2,200. Luke dies at 83 (i.e., in the month of his 83rd birthday) and Sara dies at 95.

In Strategy 1, Sara begins benefits based on her earnings record at 62 and receives $750 a month. When Luke reaches FRA, he applies for spousal benefits only and receives $500 a month. At 70, he switches to benefits based on his earnings record and receives $2,904 a month, and the lower earner switches to spousal benefits of $850, that is, $750 (own benefit at 62) + ($1,100 - $1,000), where $1,100 is her spousal benefits at FRA or later and $1,000 is benefits based on her earnings record at FRA. After his death, she gets survivor's benefits of $2,904 a month.

In Strategy 2, Sara begins benefits based on her earnings record when he attains FRA and receives $933 a month. At that time, Luke applies for spousal benefits only and receives $500 a month. At 70, he switches to benefits based on his earnings record and receives $2,904 a month, and the lower earner switches to spousal benefits of $1,033, that is, $933 (own benefit at 65) + ($1,100 - $1,000), where $1,100 is her spousal benefits at FRA or later and $1,000 is benefits based on her earnings record at FRA. After his death, she gets survivor's benefits of $2,904 a month.

In Strategy 3, Luke files and suspends his benefits sometime between when he reaches FRA and Sara reaches FRA. Since Luke has filed for benefits, Sara is eligible to file for spousal benefits only at her FRA and receive $1,100 a month. When Luke turns 70, he begins benefits at $2,904. At 70, she switches to benefits based on her earnings record and receives $1,320, which reflects 32% delayed retirement credits. After Luke's death, Sara gets survivor's benefits of $2,904 a month.

In Strategy 4, when she attains FRA, Sara files for benefits based on her earnings record and receives $1,000 a month, which makes Luke eligible to apply for spousal benefits of $500 a month. He gets three years of spousal benefits from age 67 through 69. At 70, Luke switches to benefits based on his earnings record and receives $2,904 a month, and Sara adds spousal benefits for a combined retirement/spousal benefit of $1,100 a month, half of his PIA. After his death, she gets survivor's benefits of $2,904 a month.

In Strategy 62, they both begin benefits at age 62. At 62, Luke gets benefits of $1,650 a month. One year later, Sara turns 62 and files for benefits. She receives $820 a month in combined retirement plus spousal benefits, [0.75($1,000) + 0.7($1,100 - $1,000)], where $1,000 is her PIA, $1,100 is her base spousal benefit and 0.75 and 0.7 reflect the reductions in her own benefits and spousal benefits for starting benefits 48 month before attaining FRA. After his death, she gets survivor's benefits of $1,815 a month, which is 82.5% of his PIA.

Table 4.7 presents Sara and Luke's cumulative lifetime benefits for various combinations of dates of death for each partner. The following lessons apply. First, if both partners die at young ages, Strategy 62 usually provides the highest cumulative benefits as shown in S73/L73. Second, in every other case at least one partner lives well past the age that the higher earner turns 80. So, the couple's cumulative lifetime benefits are much larger in Strategies 1 through 4 than in Strategy 62. Third, notice that in Strategy 1, the lower earner begins benefits at 62, while in Strategies 2, 3, and 4, she waits until a later date to begin receiving benefits. Therefore, it should not be surprising that Strategy 1 usually provides the largest lifetime benefits when one partner dies before the lower earning spouse turns 80 as in S95/L73 and S75/L83. Fourth, if both partners live long lives as in S95/L93, cumulative benefits are usually maximized in Strategy 3 because this strategy maximizes their combined monthly benefits once both partners have attained age 70.

Table 4.7.	Cumulative Lifetime Benefits for a Medium Ratio Couple				
Ages of Death	**Strategy 1**	**Strategy 2**	**Strategy 3**	**Strategy 4**	**Strategy 62**
S95/L73	**$1,023,648**	$1,012,020	$990,528	$999,648	$817,140
S95/L83	1,125,648	1,135,980	**1,148,928**	1,131,648	895,740
S95/L93	1,227,648	1,259,940	**1,307,328**	1,263,648	974,340
S85/L83	777,168	787,500	**800,448**	783,168	677,940
S75/L83	**601,224**	596,184	585,024	586,224	557,580
S73/L73	256,992	245,364	223,872	232,992	**337,980**

S95/L73 indicates that Sara dies at 95 and Luke dies at 73. Bold denotes the largest cumulative lifetime benefits.

Couple Example 10, Medium Low Ratio couple: Assuming an FRA of 66 for the younger spouse, the Medium Low Ratio group has a ratio of low-to-high PIAs that is greater than 0.333 and less than 0.379.

Table 4.8 presents the monthly Social Security benefits for Wanda and Harry, a Medium Low Ratio couple, for various claiming strategies assuming that she dies at 95 and he dies at 73. Harry is 62 with a PIA of $2,200. Wanda is 59 with a PIA of $800. They both have FRAs of 66. They are a Medium Low ratio couple because $800/$2,200 falls between 0.333 and 0.379.

Table 4.8.	Combined Monthly Benefits from Four Strategies for a Medium Low Ratio Couple			
Wanda/ Harry's Ages	Strategy 1	Strategy 2	Strategy 3	Strategy 62
59/62				$1650
60/63				1650
61/64				1650
62/65	$600			810+1650
63/66	600+400	640+400		810+1650
64/67	600+400	640+400		810+1650
65/68	600+400	640+400		810+1650
66/69	600+400	640+400	$800+400	810+1650
67/70	900+2904	940+2904	1100+2904	810+1650
68/71	900+2904	940+2904	1100+2904	810+1650
69/72	900+2904	940+2904	1100+2904	810+1650
70/	2904	2904	2904	1815
71/	2904	2904	2904	1815
72/	2904	2904	2904	1815
...	...	...	...	
94/	2904	2904	2904	1815
Cum Lifetime Benefits	$1,063,344	$1,059,504	$1,029,744	$840,060

Wanda is 59 with Primary Insurance Amount of $800 and Harry is 62 with PIA of $2,200. Harry dies at 73 (i.e., in the month of his 73rd birthday) and Wanda dies at 95.

In Strategy 1, Wanda begins benefits based on her earnings record at 62 and receives $600 a month. One year later Harry attains FRA and applies for spousal benefits of $400 a month. At 70, he switches to benefits based on his earnings record of $2,904 a month, and she adds spousal benefits of $300 to her $600 monthly retirement benefit, that is, $1,100

- $800, where $1,100 is her base spousal benefit and $800 is her PIA. After Harry's death, Wanda receives survivor's benefits of $2,904 a month.

In Strategy 2, Wanda begins benefits based on her earnings record when Harry attains FRA and receives $640 a month. At that time, Harry files for spousal benefits only and receives $400 a month. At 70, Harry switches to his benefits based on his earnings record and receives $2,904 a month, while Wanda adds spousal benefits of $300 and thus receives $940 a month, that is, $640 (her own benefits at 63) + ($1,100 - $800), where $1,100 is her base spousal benefit and $800 is her PIA. After Harry's death, Wanda gets survivor's benefits of $2,904 a month.

In Strategy 3, Wanda files for benefits based only on her earnings record at FRA and receives $800 a month, which makes Harry eligible to apply for spousal benefits only of $400 a month. In this example, Harry only gets one year of spousal benefits because Wanda does not file for benefits until Harry is 69. When he turns 70, Harry switches to benefits based on his earnings record and receives $2,904 a month, while Wanda switches to spousal benefits of $1,100 a month. After his death, she gets survivor's benefits of $2,904 a month.

In Strategy 62, they both begin benefits at age 62. At 62, Harry gets benefits of $1,650 a month. Three years later, Wanda turns 62 and begins benefits of $810; benefits based on her record are 75% of $800 and spousal benefits are 70% of ($1,100 - $800), where $800 is her PIA, $1,100 in her base spousal benefit, and 75% and 70% reflect reduced benefits based on her record and reduced spousal benefits for beginning benefits 48 months early. After Harry's death, Wanda gets survivor's benefits of $1,815 a month, which is 82.5% of his PIA.

Table 4.9 presents this couple's cumulative lifetime benefits for various combinations of dates of death for each partner. The following lessons apply. First, if both partners die at very young ages, Strategy 62 usually provides the highest cumulative benefits as shown in W73/H73. Second, in every other case at least one partner lives well past the age that the higher earner turns 80. So, the couple's cumulative lifetime benefits are much larger in Strategies 1 through 3 than in Strategy 62. Third, in Strategies 1 and 2, the lower earner begins benefits before FRA, while in Strategy 3 she waits until FRA to begin receiving benefits. Therefore, Strategy 1 or 2 usually provides the largest lifetime benefits when one partner dies before the lower earning spouse turns 80 as in W95/H73 and W75/H83, while Strategy 3 usually provides the largest cumulative benefits if both partners live long lives as in W95/H93. In this example, Strategy 2 provides the largest cumulative benefits—and it is a small advantage at that—if the first spouse dies sometime between when the lower earner is 78 to 84.

Table 4.9.	Cumulative Lifetime Benefits for a Medium Low Ratio Couple			
Ages of Death	**Strategy 1**	**Strategy 2**	**Strategy 3**	**Strategy 62**
W95/H73	**$1,063,344**	$1,059,504	$1,029,744	$840,060
W95/H83	1,171,344	**1,172,304**	1,161,744	917,460
W95/H93	1,279,344	1,285,104	**1,293,744**	994,860
W85/H83	822,864	**823,824**	813,264	699,660
W75/H83	**594,624**	593,184	573,024	552,060
W73/H73	296,688	292,848	263,088	**360,900**

W95/H73 indicates that Wanda dies at age 95 and Harry dies at 73. Bold denotes the largest cumulative lifetime benefits.

It is instructive to compare the cash flows of Strategies 1, 2, and 3. As noted earlier, one of these strategies is the best when one partner lives well past the age the higher earner turns 80. The pattern of cash flows indicates that Strategy 1 provides the largest cumulative benefits if the first spouse to die does so at a young age. Strategy 2 provides the largest cumulative benefits if the first spouse to die lives to about average age, while Strategy 3 provides the largest cumulative benefit if the first spouse to die lives well beyond average life expectancy. In this example, the exact breakeven age between Strategies 1 and 2 is when the younger spouse turns 78, while the breakeven age between Strategies 2 and 3 is about 85. Although the exact breakeven ages vary among couples, the relative appeal of Strategies 1 through 3 depends on the life expectancy of the first spouse to die for other Medium Low Ratio couples. In a related point, Strategy 3 has the largest combined monthly benefit while both partners are alive after the higher earner attains age 70. So, this strategy also minimizes their longevity risk if both partners live long lives.

Couple Example 11, Low Ratio couple: The Low Ratio group has a ratio of low-to-high PIAs that is less than or equal to 0.333.

Table 4.10 presents the monthly Social Security benefits for Wendy and Hugh, a Low Ratio couple, assuming Wendy is 59 with a PIA of $500 and Hugh is 62 with a PIA of $2,200. It assumes she dies at 95 and he at 73. They both have FRAs of 66. They are a Low Ratio couple because the $500/$2,200 is less than or equal to 0.333.

Table 4.10.	Combined Monthly Benefits from Six Strategies for a Low Ratio Couple					
Wendy/ Hugh's Ages	Strategy 1	Strategy 2	Strategy 3	Strategy 4	Strategy 5	Strategy 62
59/62						$1650
60/63						1650
61/64						1650
62/65	$375	$375		$375		795+1650
63/66	825	375	$400+250	375+250		795+1650
64/67	825	375	$400+250	375+250		795+1650
65/68	825	375	$400+250	375+250		795+1650
66/69	825	975	$400+250	375+250	$1100	795+1650
67/70	825+2904	975+2904	1000+2904	975+2904	1100+2904	795+1650
68/71	825+2904	975+2904	1000+2904	975+2904	1100+2904	795+1650
69/72	825+2904	975+2904	1000+2904	975+2904	1100+2904	795+1650
70/	2904	2904	2904	2904	2904	1815
71/	2904	2904	2904	2904	2904	1815
72/	2904	2904	2904	2904	2904	1815
...	...	...	...	...	...	
94/	2904	2904	2904	2904	2904	1815
Cum Lifetime Benefits	$1,049,544	$1,040,544	$1,042,944	$1,045,344	$1,028,544	$838,620

Wendy is 59 with Primary Insurance Amount of $500 and Hugh is 62 with PIA of $2,200. Hugh dies at 73 (i.e., in the month of his 73rd birthday) and Wendy dies at 95.

In Strategy 1, Wendy begins benefits based on her earnings record at 62 and receives $375 a month. She is not yet eligible for spousal benefits. In one year, Hugh attains FRA and files and suspends his benefits, while Wendy begins spousal benefits at that time. She receives $825 a month = $375 (own benefits at 62) + 75%($1,100 - $500), where $1,100 is her base spousal benefit, $500 is her PIA, and 75% reflects her reduced spousal benefits at age 63. At 70, Hugh begins benefits based on his record and receives $2,904 a month. After his death, Wendy gets $2,904 a month in survivor's benefits for the rest of her life.

In Strategy 2, Wendy begins benefits based on her earnings record at 62 and receives $375. She is not yet eligible for spousal benefits. Sometime between when Hugh attains FRA and Wendy attains FRA, Hugh files and suspends his benefits. At her FRA, Wendy adds spousal benefits. She receives $975, that is, $375 (her own benefits at 62) + ($1,100 - $500), where $1,100 is her spousal benefits at FRA or later and $500 is benefits based on her earnings record if begun at FRA. At 70, Hugh begins benefits based on his earnings record and receives $2,904 a month. After his death, Wendy gets $2,904 a month in survivor's benefits for the rest of her life.

In Strategy 3, Wendy begins benefits based on her earnings record when Hugh attains FRA; Wendy receives $400 a month. At the same time, Hugh files for spousal benefits only and receives $250 a month, half of Wendy's PIA. At 70, he switches to benefits based on his record, increasing his benefit to $2,904 a month, and Wendy adds spousal benefits for a combined retirement/spousal benefit of $1,000, that is, $400 (her own benefits at 63) + ($1,100 - $500). After Hugh's death, Wendy collects survivor's benefits of $2,904 a month.

In Strategy 4, Wendy begins benefits based on her earnings record at 62 and receives $375 a month. One year later Hugh attains FRA and applies for spousal benefits only of $250 a month. At 70, he switches to benefits based on his record and receives $2,904 a month, and Wendy adds spousal benefits for a combined retirement/spousal benefit of $975, that is, $375 (her own benefits at 62) + ($1,100 - $500). After his death, she gets survivor's benefits of $2,904 a month. After his death, she gets survivor's benefits of $2,904 a month.

In Strategy 5, Hugh files and suspends his benefits sometime between the time he attains FRA and Wendy attains FRA. This makes Wendy eligible for spousal benefits of $1,100 a month when she files for benefits at her FRA. When he turns 70, Hugh begins benefits based on his record and receives $2,904. After his death, Wendy gets survivor's benefits of $2,904 a month.

In Strategy 62, they both begin benefits at age 62. At 62, Hugh receives benefits of $1,650 a month. Three years later, Wendy turns 62 and begins combined retirement/spousal benefits of $795, that is, 75%($500) + 70%($1,100 - $500), where $1,100 is her base spousal benefit, $500 is her PIA, and 75% and 70% reflect the reductions for beginning her own and spousal benefits 48 months early. After his death, she gets survivor's benefits of $1,815 a month, which is 82.5% of his PIA.

Let's first compare Strategies 1 and 2. When Hugh turns FRA and Wendy is 63, he could file and suspend his benefits, which would make her eligible for spousal benefits at that time. However, even if he files and suspends at his FRA, she could delay switching to spousal benefits until she turns FRA. In Strategy 1, Wendy switches to spousal benefits at 63, while in Strategy 2 she switches at her FRA. For this couple, Strategy 2 never provides the maximum cumulative benefits, but it can especially if one partner has a very low PIA. Therefore, it is important to understand that Wendy does not have to switch to spousal benefits when Hugh attains FRA. It sometimes pays for her to delay this switch until her FRA.

Table 4.11 presents this couple's cumulative lifetime benefits for various combinations of dates of death for each partner. The following lessons apply. First, if both partners die at young ages, Strategy 62 usually provides the highest cumulative benefits as shown in W73/H73. Second, in every other case at least one partner lives well past the age that the higher earner turns 80. So, the couple's cumulative lifetime benefits are much larger in Strategies 1 through 5 than in Strategy 62. For example, for W95/H73 the cumulative benefits in Strategies 1 through 5 are at least

$241,000 more than in Strategy 62. Third, in Strategies 1 through 4, the lower earner begins benefits before FRA, while in Strategies 5 she waits until FRA to begin receiving benefits. Therefore, Strategy 1, 2, 3, or 4 usually provides the largest cumulative lifetime benefits when one partner dies before the lower-earning spouse turns 80 as in W95/H73 and W75/H83, while Strategy 5 usually provides the largest cumulative benefits if both partners live long lives as in W95/H93. In a related point, Strategy 5 has the largest combined monthly benefit while both partners are alive after the higher earner attains age 70. So, this strategy also minimizes their longevity risk if both partners live long lives.

Table 4.11.	Cumulative Lifetime Benefits for a Low Ratio Couple					
Ages of Death	Strategy 1	Strategy 2	Strategy 3	Strategy 4	Strategy 5	Strategy 62
W95/H73	**$1,049,544**	$1,040,544	$1,042,944	$1,045,344	$1,028,544	$838,620
W95/H83	1,148,544	1,157,544	**1,162,944**	1,162,344	1,160,544	914,220
W95/H93	1,247,544	1,274,555	1,282,944	1,279,344	**1,292,544**	989,820
W85/H83	800,064	809,064	**814,464**	813,864	812,064	696,420
W75/H83	576,324	576,324	580,224	**581,124**	571,824	539,820
W73/H73	282,888	273,888	276,288	278,688	261,888	**359,460**

W95/H73 indicates that Wendy dies at 95 and Hugh dies at 73. Bold denotes the largest cumulative lifetime benefits.

Guidance if at least one spouse dies early: Finally, we provide guidance for situations where at least one partner dies before age 75. If at least one partner dies early, the strategy that maximizes cumulative lifetime benefits is sometimes Strategy 62, where both partners begin benefits as soon as possible. However, Strategy 1 as described below sometimes provides the largest cumulative benefits. In addition, Strategy 5 for the High Ratio group occasionally provides the largest cumulative benefits. So, when the couple is not a High-Ratio couple, Strategies 62 and 1 should be considered when one spouse is expected to die early. When the couple is a High-Ratio couple, Strategies 62, 1, and 5 should be considered when one spouse is expected to die early.

In Strategy 1, the lower earner begins benefits based on her record at 62. The higher earner, if alive, begins spousal benefits at his FRA and, if alive, switches to benefits based on his record at age 70. Suppose the higher earner dies at his FRA or earlier, then the younger spouse will continue her benefits until attaining her FRA for survivor's benefits and then switch to survivor's benefits.

Occasionally, Strategy 5 of the High Ratio group provides the largest cumulative lifetime benefits, especially if it is a High Ratio couple and the higher earner dies at or before his FRA. In Strategy 5, the higher earner begins benefits on his record at 62, and the lower earner begins spousal benefits at her FRA (if her husband is still alive) and switches to her own benefits at 70. Suppose the higher earner dies at FRA or earlier. Then the surviving spouse of the High Ratio couple begins survivor's benefits and switches to the higher benefits based on her earnings record at 70.

In general, if both partners die before their mid-70s, Strategy 62 usually provides the largest cumulative lifetime benefits. If the surviving partner lives beyond his or her mid-70s, Strategy 1 usually provides the largest cumulative lifetime benefits. Furthermore, Strategy 1 provides the largest benefit at age 70 and beyond for the surviving spouse. So, this strategy also minimizes longevity risk.

Recommended Strategies for Surviving Spouses

This section presents guidelines that should help financial advisors quickly determine the best strategy for a widow or widower who is eligible for survivor's benefits. It presents summary advice for four Groups of clients that vary in terms of the age of the surviving spouse. For clarity, we assume the wife is the surviving spouse, but the logic is the same if the husband is the surviving spouse. Group 1 includes widows who are 70 or older. Group 2 includes widows who are between their FRA for survivor's benefits and age 70. Groups 3 and 4 include surviving spouses who are younger than their FRAs for survivor's benefits. Group 3 includes widows who have the lower PIA, while Group 4 includes widows who have the higher PIA.

Group 1: In Group 1, the surviving spouse is age 70 or older when the first spouse dies. This is the largest group since most of the time the surviving spouse will be 70 or older when her spouse dies. The advice is simple. The surviving spouse should take the larger of her own benefits or her survivor's benefits. This benefit level will continue for the rest of her life.

It is harder to determine the best strategy for the surviving spouse in Groups 2 through 4. One key is that *the surviving widow's benefits based on her earnings record continue to receive delayed retirement credits until they are begun.* As we shall she, this sometimes provides better strategies than simply taking the higher of her own benefits and her deceased spouse's benefits.

Group 2: In Group 2, the surviving spouse is at least FRA for survivor's benefits but less than 70. If the higher earner dies then the surviving spouse should begin survivor's benefits and at 70 switch to her own benefits if higher. This is an easy decision. For example, suppose she is 66, has a PIA of $1,800 and FRA for survivor's benefits of 66 when her husband dies. Assume he began benefits based on his record at or after FRA and was receiving $2,000 a month. Her best claiming strategy is to begin survivor's benefits of $2,000 a month and at 70 switch to her own benefits of $2,376. In another strategy, she could begin receiving benefits of $1,800 a month at his death based on her earnings record and later switch to survivor's benefits of $2,000. The latter strategy would provide less money for all time horizons.

If the lower earner dies, the best decision is not as clear. Suppose she has a PIA of $2,000 and is 66 (her FRA for all benefits). He began benefits based on his record at or after FRA and dies while receiving $1,600 a month. In Strategy 1, she begins survivor's benefits of $1,600 today at 66 and switches at 70 to benefits based on her earnings record of $2,640 a month. In Strategy 2, she begins benefits based on her record today of $2,000 and it continues at this level through the years. If she dies before age 72.5, Strategy 2 provides the larger cumulative benefits. Otherwise, Strategy 1 provides the larger cumulative benefits. From Lesson 1, the cumulative value of $2,000 a month from age 66 to 80 is approximately equal to the cumulative value of $2,640 a month from age 70 to 80. So, the additional $1,600 a month in survivor's benefits from 66 through 69 is like a free good. Although the precise breakeven age varies with the sizes of the two PIAs, Strategy 1 always provides the larger cumulative benefit unless the surviving widow dies at an unusually young age. Furthermore, Strategy 1 does a better job of reducing her longevity risk because it provides the larger monthly benefit at age 70 and beyond.

If the surviving spouse has already started benefits, it sometimes pays for her to repay prior benefits, start survivor's benefits, and switch at 70 to her own benefits. As before, suppose she is 66 with a PIA of $2,000 when he dies while receiving $1,600 a month. Furthermore, suppose she started benefits based on her earnings record of $1,933 a month six months earlier at age 65 years and six months and withdrew those benefits after receiving benefits through age 65 and 11 months. Example 2 in Table 4.12 compares two of her claiming strategies. In Strategy 1, she continues her own benefits of $1,933 a month since this is larger than her survivor's benefits. In Strategy 2, she uses the do-over option. She repays prior benefits of about $11,598. She starts survivor's benefits of $1,600 a month and switches at 70 to her own benefits of $2,640 a month. If she lives beyond about 73.5 then Strategy 2 would provide the larger cumulative benefit. In addition, since Strategy 2 provides the larger monthly benefit from age 70 and beyond, it minimizes her longevity risk. NOTE: An ex-Social Security agent advised us that the claimant will have to request this option. She believes it is highly unlikely that the agent will think of this strategy even though it is legal.

The key to these strategies is that benefits based on her earnings record continue to receive delayed retirement credits until begun. Depending on her PIA and his benefits level, it is sometimes better to take survivor's benefits and then switch to her own benefits at 70, where the latter reflects delayed retirement credits.

Table 4.12.	Group 2 Examples, Widow is at Least FRA for Survivor's Benefits but Younger than 70					
	Example 1			Example 2		
Age	Strategy 1	Strategy 2	Difference (S2 - S1)	Strategy 1	Strategy 2	Difference (S2 - S1)
					-$11,598	-$11,598
66	$1600	$2000	$4800	$1933	$1600	-15,594
67	1600	2000	9600	1933	1600	-19,590
68	1600	2000	14400	1933	1600	-23,586
69	1600	2000	19200	1933	1600	-27,582
70	2640	2000	11520	1933	2640	-19,098
71	2640	2000	3840	1933	2640	-10,614
72	2640	2000	-3840	1933	2640	-2,130
73	2640	2000	-11520	1933	2640	6,354
74	2640	2000	-19200	1933	2640	14,838

In Example 1, the widow is 66 with a Primary Insurance Amount of $2,000 when her husband dies. Her FRA for survivor's benefits is 66 and her survivor's benefit based on her husband's record is $1,600. In Example 2, her PIA is $2,000 and her survivor's benefit at his death is $1,600 a month. She began benefits based on her record six months ago at age 65 and six months of $1,933 a month. She repays these benefits, starts survivor's benefits at 66 and switches to benefits based on her earnings record at 70. Except for −$11,598, which is a one-time payment, the Strategy columns show monthly totals, while the Difference (S2 − S1) column shows cumulative benefits of Strategy 2 less cumulative benefits of Strategy 1. A positive value indicates that Strategy 2 provides higher cumulative benefits, and vice versa.

Group 3: In Group 3, the surviving spouse is younger than her FRA for survivor's benefits and the spouse with the higher PIA dies. For example, she may be 60 with a PIA of $1,600 and FRA for survivor's benefits of 66, when her husband dies while receiving $2,000 a month. From Table 4.13, in Strategy 1 of Example 1 she begins her own benefits at 62 of $1,200 a month and switches at FRA for survivor's benefits to survivor's benefits of

$2,000 a month. In Strategy 2, she begins survivor's benefits at 60 of $1,430 a month and switches to her own benefits at 70 of $2,112 a month. The column labeled Difference (S2 - S1) shows cumulative benefits to Strategy 2 less cumulative benefits to Strategy 1. In Example 1, Strategy 2 provides the larger cumulative benefits no matter how long the surviving spouse lives.

Table 4.13.		Group 3 Examples, Widow is Younger than FRA for Survivor's Benefits and is the Lower Earner				
	Example 1			Example 2		
Age	Strategy 1	Strategy 2	Difference (S2 - S1)	Strategy 1	Strategy 2	Difference (S2 - S1)
60		$1430	$17,160		$1430	$17,160
61		1430	34,320		1430	34,320
62	$1200	1430	37,080	$600	1430	44,280
63	1200	1430	39,840	600	1430	54,240
64	1200	1430	42,600	600	1430	64,200
65	1200	1430	45,360	600	1430	74,160
66	2000	1430	38,520	2000	1430	67,320
67	2000	1430	31,680	2000	1430	60,480
68	2000	1430	24,840	2000	1430	53,640
69	2000	1430	18,000	2000	1430	46,800
70	2000	2112	19,344	2000	1430	39,960
71	2000	2112	20,688	2000	1430	33,120
72	2000	2112	22,032	2000	1430	26,280
73	2000	2112	23,376	2000	1430	19,440
74	2000	2112	24,720	2000	1430	12,600
75	2000	2112	26,064	2000	1430	5,760
76	2000	2112	27,408	2000	1430	-1,080
77	2000	2112	28,752	2000	1430	-7,920

In Example 1, the widow is 60 with a Primary Insurance Amount of $1,600 when her husband dies while receiving $2,000 a month. Example 2 repeats Example 1 except she has a PIA of $800. Her Full Retirement Age for survivor's benefits is 66. The Strategy columns show monthly totals, while the Difference (S2 - S1) columns show cumulative benefits of Strategy 2 less cumulative benefits of Strategy 1. Positive values indicate that Strategy 2 provides higher cumulative benefits, and vice versa.

Although not shown in a table, consider the example above except suppose the surviving widow is age 63 when her husband dies, and she had already begun her own benefits within the prior year. In this case, she should consider the do-over option. It may pay for her to repay prior benefits, start survivor's benefits, and switch at 70 to her own benefits. The key is she can get the higher benefit of $2,112 a month beginning at age 70.

Example 2 in Table 4.13 repeats Example 1, except it assumes her PIA is $800. In Strategy 1, she begins her own benefits of $600 a month at 62 and switches to survivor's benefits at FRA for survivor's benefits of $2,000 a month. In Strategy 2, she begins survivor's benefits of $1,430 a month at 60. The Difference (S2 - S1) column shows cumulative benefits to Strategy 2 less cumulative benefits to Strategy 1. It turns negative when she is 76, indicating that Strategy 1 provides the larger cumulative benefits if she lives past her mid-70s. The reductions in benefits for starting survivor's benefits before FRA are approximately actuarially fair assuming the surviving spouse lives to about age 81. That is, the cumulative benefits through age 81 of $1,430 a month starting at age 60 is about the same as that of $2,000 a month starting at age 66. Strategy 1 provides $2,000 a month beginning at 66 plus an additional $600 a month from ages 62 to 66. This $600 a month is like a free good. Consequently, Strategy 1 usually provides the larger cumulative lifetime benefits unless the surviving spouse has a shorter-than-average lifetime. In addition, since Strategy 1 provides the larger payment from her FRA for survivor's benefits onward, this strategy also minimizes her longevity risk.

Next, consider a survivor who has not worked enough to qualify for benefits based on her own record. In this case, two of her claiming strategies would be to begin survivor's benefits as soon as possible or to delay survivor's benefits until she attains FRA for survivor's benefits. The reductions in survivor's benefits are set to be approximately actuarially fair for someone with an average lifespan. So, the cumulative lifetime benefits, assuming she lives to her early 80s, are approximately the same whether she starts survivor's benefits at age 60, 61, 62, or any age through her FRA for survivors. If she has a short life expectancy, she may want to start survivor's benefits as soon as possible. If she has an average or longer-than-average life expectancy, she will probably want to delay benefits until FRA for survivor's benefits since this strategy provides a similar sized or larger expected cumulative benefit while also minimizing her longevity risk should she live a long life.

Group 4: In In Group 4, the surviving spouse is younger than her FRA for survivor's benefits and the spouse with the lower PIA dies. The difference between Groups 3 and 4 is whether the spouse with the higher or lower PIA dies. Suppose she is 62 with a PIA of $2,000 and FRA for survivor's benefits of 66. He had a PIA of $1,200, but began his benefits at $900 a month at age 62. He dies. Table 4.14 compares two of her claiming strategies. In Strategy 1, she begins benefits based on her earnings record at 62 of $1,500 a month. In Strategy 2, she begins survivor's benefits of $972 a month. Since he began benefits before FRA and she began survivor's benefits before FRA, her survivor's benefits depend on the sequence of three amounts: the deceased's retirement benefit of $900, 82.5% of his PIA or $990, and her reduced widow's insurance benefits of 81% of his PIA or $972, where 81% reflects the 19% reduction percentage for beginning survivor's benefits at age 62. These numbers follow Sequence 5, so her survivor's benefit is $972 a month. She switches to benefits based on her record of $2,640 a month at 70. The key to understanding why Strategy 2 usually fares better is to recall Lesson 1. The breakeven age for $1,500 a month beginning at 62 and $2,640 a month beginning at 70 is about age 80. Therefore, Strategy 2 provides the $2,640 a month beginning at 70 plus an additional $972 a month from age 62 through 69. This additional $972 a month is like a free good. The Difference (S2 - S1) column shows the cumulative benefits advantage of Strategy 2 compared to Strategy 1. Strategy 2 provides the larger cumulative benefits shortly after she turns 73. The exact breakeven age varies but, because Strategy 2 provides the "free" $972 a month, it provides the larger cumulative lifetime benefits for most widows. In addition, Strategy 2 provides the larger monthly payment from age 70 onward. So, it minimizes her longevity risk.

Table 4.14.	Group 4 Example, Widow is Younger than FRA for Survivor's Benefits and is the Higher Earner		
Age	Strategy 1	Strategy 2	Difference (S2 - S1)
62	$1500	$972	-$6,336
63	1500	972	-12,672
64	1500	972	-19,008
65	1500	972	-25,344
66	1500	972	-31,680
67	1500	972	-38,016
68	1500	972	-44,352
69	1500	972	-50,688
70	1500	2640	-37,008
71	1500	2640	-23,328
72	1500	2640	-9,648
73	1500	2640	4,032
74	1500	2640	17,712
75	1500	2640	31,392
76	1500	2640	45,072

The widow is 62 with a Primary Insurance Amount of $2,000 when her husband dies. In Strategy 1, she begins her own benefits at 62 of $1,500 a month and continues these benefits. In Strategy 2, she begins survivor's benefit at age 62 of $972 a month. See "Rules governing survivor's benefits" for a discussion of the rules determining this amount. At 70, she switches to her own benefits of $2,640 a month, which reflects her delayed retirement credits. The Strategy columns show monthly totals, while the Difference (S2 - S1) column shows cumulative benefits of Strategy 2 less cumulative benefits of Strategy 1. A positive value indicates that Strategy 2 provides the higher cumulative benefits, and vice versa.

Although not shown in the table, if the surviving spouse has begun benefits based on her record within the prior year, she should consider the do-over option. It may pay for her to repay prior benefits, start survivors benefits, and switch at 70 to her own benefits. The key is her benefits at 70 and beyond will be much higher due to the delayed retirement credits.

In summary, the best strategy for a surviving widow depends upon her age. In addition, it sometimes depends upon a) the relative sizes of her PIA and her deceased husband's benefits level, and b) the widow's projected lifetime. Based on the examples in this section, a financial advisor should be able to quickly help a widow or widower make an informed decision about the best claiming strategy for the situation. For more information concerning widow(er)s in Groups 3 and 4, see the article by Shuart, Weaver, and Whitman.[12]

Summary

This chapter presented strategies for couples who are deciding when to begin Social Security benefits. This is the longest chapter and the most difficult material in this book. Although strategies for married couples are more complex than strategies for singles, there is also more opportunity to add value to couples by helping them decide when each partner should begin benefits.

We began this chapter with explanations of spousal benefits and survivor's benefits because these benefits are often keys when deciding when each partner should begin Social Security benefits. In particular, we presented two very important lessons that apply specifically to couples' claiming strategies. Lessons 2 and 3 from this chapter, combined with Lesson 1 from Chapter 3, are keys to understanding couples' claiming strategies.

Lesson 2	The relevant life expectancy for the decision of when the spouse with the higher PIA should begin benefits based on his earnings record is the lifetime of the second spouse to die, while the relevant life expectancy for the decision as to when the spouse with the lower PIA should begin benefits based on her record is the lifetime of the first spouse to die.

---

12 Amy N. Shuart, David A. Weaver, and Kevin Whitman, "Widowed Before Retirement: Social Security Benefit Claiming Strategies," *Journal of Financial Planning*, April 2010.

Lesson 3 | If at least one spouse lives well beyond the age that the higher earner turns 80, the couple's cumulative lifetime benefits will usually be highest if he delays benefits based on his record until age 70.

We presented several examples that illustrated that a couple's claiming strategy is important. Indeed, the best claiming strategy may add several hundred thousand dollars in lifetime benefits. The examples also illustrated Lessons 2 and 3, and explained key insights determining when each partner should begin Social Security benefits. We provided a detailed example for each of four couples groups, where each couples group is defined based on the ratio of the partners' low-to-high Primary Insurance Amounts. For each group, we compared the couple's cumulative lifetime benefits for several claiming strategies for various life expectancies of each partner. Finally, we described recommended strategies for surviving spouses after the death of their partner.

For those who choose to utilize the available complementing software, much of the analysis for a particular situation is completed automatically, and clients are able to see their options graphically and select the strategy that best suits their needs. However, given the information in this chapter, an advisor should be able to collect appropriate information from clients and be able to quickly zero in on one or two good claiming strategies that are well-suited for that married couple to consider. Perhaps the most important role is for the financial advisor to be comfortable explaining the pros and cons of each strategy so clients can make an informed decision about their claiming strategy.

CHAPTER 5
Nontraditional Situations and Detailed Rules You Should Know

This chapter highlights nontraditional, but not uncommon, situations advisors will face with clients. We've also included a set of details that are vital to understand when crafting strategies for some clients. The nontraditional situations and detailed rules are significant pieces to the Social Security puzzle for the clients they affect and can materially impact their choice of an optimal strategy.

For someone insured by Social Security, other individuals such as a widow(er), a divorced widow(er), unmarried minor children, disabled children, and parents may be eligible to receive benefits based on the insured's earnings record. The availability of other benefits, children's benefits for example, can affect when a single parent or each partner in a couple chooses to begin Social Security benefits. We also present examples that explain how a pension from work not covered by Social Security would affect benefits. We will briefly discuss divorced spouse's benefits and disability benefits, and we present information on the earnings test, the do-over option, and timing issues associated with certain benefits.

Children's Benefits

The following information has been taken directly from the Social Security Administration's website and appears as a direct quote from that site.

"When you qualify for Social Security retirement benefits, your children may also qualify to receive benefits on your record. Your eligible child can be your biological child, adopted child or stepchild. A dependent grandchild may also qualify.

"To receive benefits, the child must:

- be unmarried; and
- be under age 18; or
- be 18-19 years old and a full-time student (no higher than grade 12); or
- be 18 or older and disabled from a disability that started before age 22.

"Normally, benefits stop when children reach age 18 unless they are disabled. However, if the child is still a full-time student at a secondary (or elementary) school at age 18, benefits will continue until the child graduates or until two months after the child becomes age 19, whichever is first.

"Benefits paid for your child will not decrease your retirement benefit. In fact, the value of the benefits he or she may receive, added to your own, may help you decide if taking your benefits sooner may be more advantageous.

"Within your family, each qualified child may receive a monthly payment up to one-half of your full retirement benefit amount. However, there is a limit to the amount we can pay your family members. The total depends on your benefit amount and the number of family members who also qualify on your record. The total varies, but generally the total amount your family can receive is about 50 to 80 percent of your full retirement benefit.

"**Note:** If you have a divorced spouse who qualifies for benefits, it will not affect the amount of benefits you or your family may receive."

For more information, see http://www.socialsecurity.gov/retire2/your-children.htm.

Example 1, Child with single parent: Table 5.1 presents an example where a single parent or grandparent is 62 years old with a PIA of $1,000 and she has a child age 14 or grandchild age 14 whom she adopted. The single parent dies at 95, that is, in the month of her 95th birthday. (In all examples, we assume benefits are received for January through December in the first year.) In Strategy 1, she begins benefits at 66, her Full Retirement Age, and receives $1,000 a month. Since her child or grandchild would then be 18 (and we assume not a full time student in grade 12 or under), he would not receive benefits. In Strategy 2, she begins her benefits today at $750 a month and her child receives half of her PIA or $500 a month for a total of $1,250 a month for the next four years. At 66, her $750 a month continues and the child's benefits cease. Strategy 2 provides a larger cumulative lifetime benefit until and if the single mother or grandmother turns 86. As discussed in Table 3.2, the breakeven age between the single person beginning benefits at 62 versus 66 is age 78 when there are no children's benefits. The additional $500 a month in child's benefits collected for four years lengthens that breakeven period until age 86. The choice between Strategies 1 and 2 depends on her need for money at 62, her expected lifetime, and her interest in reducing longevity risk. She must determine which is more important: receiving $1,000 a month for life in Strategy 1 versus receiving $1,250 a month for four years then $750 a month from age 66 onward in Strategy 2. If she has an average or shorter-than-average life expectancy then she will probably prefer to begin Social Security benefits at age 62 to capture the child's benefits.

Table 5.1.	Comparing Two Strategies for Single Parent with Child		
Mother's Age	Strategy 1	Strategy 2	Difference (in cumulative benefits)
62		$1250	$15,000
63		1250	30,000
64		1250	45,000
65		1250	60,000
66	$1000	750	57,000
67	1000	750	54,000
68	1000	750	51,000
69	1000	750	48,000
70	1000	750	45,000
71	1000	750	42,000
72	1000	750	39,000
73	1000	750	36,000
74	1000	750	33,000
75	1000	750	30,000
76	1000	750	27,000
77	1000	750	24,000
78	1000	750	21,000
79	1000	750	18,000
80	1000	750	15,000
81	1000	750	12,000
82	1000	750	9,000
83	1000	750	6,000
84	1000	750	-3,000
...	...	...	...
94	1000	750	-27,000

The single parent or grandparent is 62 with FRA of 66 and PIA of $1,000. The (grand)parent dies at 95. The child is 14 and is eligible for four years of benefits at 50% of (grand)parent's PIA. The Strategy columns show monthly totals, while the Difference column shows cumulative benefits of Strategy 2 less cumulative benefits of Strategy 1. A positive value indicates that Strategy 2 has the higher cumulative benefits, while a negative value indicates that Strategy 1 has the higher cumulative benefits.

Example 2, Child with two parents: Table 5.2 presents two strategies for parents or grandparents with one child age 14. The parents or grandparents (henceforth, assumed parents) are both 62 with FRAs of 66. The father has a PIA of $2,000, and the mother has a PIA of $1,200. We assume the father will die at 80 and the mother at 95.

Table 5.2.	Comparing Two Strategies for Couple with Child				
Ages	Strategy 1 Father's Benefits	Strategy 1 Mother & Child's Benefits	Strategy 2 Mother's Benefits	Strategy 2 Father & Child's Benefits	Difference (in cumulative benefits)
62	$1500	$1000	$900	$600	-$12,000
63	1500	1000	900	600	-24,000
64	1500	1000	900	600	-36,000
65	1500	1000	900	600	-48,000
66	1500	1000	900	600	-60,000
67	1500	1000	900	600	-72,000
68	1500	1000	900	600	-84,000
69	1500	1000	900	600	-96,000
70	1500	1584	900	2640	-90,528
71	1500	1584	900	2640	-85,056
72	1500	1584	900	2640	-79,584
73	1500	1584	900	2640	-74,112
74	1500	1584	900	2640	-68,640
75	1500	1584	900	2640	-63,168
76	1500	1584	900	2640	-57,696
77	1500	1584	900	2640	-52,224
78	1500	1584	900	2640	-46,752
79	1500	1584	900	2640	-41,280
80		1650		2640	-29,400
81		1650		2640	-17,520
82		1650		2640	-5,640
83		1650		2640	6,240
...		...		...	...
94		1650		2640	136,920

The father and mother are both 62 with FRAs of 66. He has a PIA of $2,000 and her PIA is $1,200. He dies at 80 and she dies at 95. Their child is 14 and is eligible for four years of benefits at 50% of parent's PIA. The Strategy columns show monthly totals, while the Difference column shows cumulative benefits of Strategy 2 less cumulative benefits of Strategy 1. A positive value indicates that Strategy 2 has the higher cumulative benefits, while a negative value indicates that Strategy 1 has the higher cumulative benefits.

In claiming Strategy 1, the father begins benefits of $1,500 a month at 62 and his daughter gets $1,000 a month, half of his PIA. At 66, the mother files for spousal benefits only and receives $1,000 a month, while their daughter turns 18 and her benefits cease. At 70, the mother switches to her own benefits of $1,584, which reflects delayed retirement credits. After he dies, the surviving widow gets $1,650 a month in survivor's benefits as explained in Case 6 in "Rules governing survivor's benefits."

In Strategy 2, the mother begins benefits of $900 a month at 62 based on her earnings record, and her daughter gets $600 a month. At 66, the father files for spousal benefits only of $600 a month, while their daughter turns 18 and her benefits cease. At 70, the father switches to his benefits of $2,640, which reflects delayed retirement credits. After the first partner dies, the surviving spouse gets the higher $2,640 a month.

Strategy 2 provides a larger cumulative lifetime benefit after about 21.5 years. It is helpful to compare the additional benefits beyond those that would go to a single individual who lives to age 80. In Strategy 1, the daughter gets $1,000 a month, half of his PIA, until she turns 18. In this example, this $1,000 a month lasts four years. In addition, the mother gets $1,000 a month beginning at FRA by applying for spousal benefits only before switching to her higher benefits at 70. In Strategy 2, the daughter gets $600 a month, half of the mother's PIA, until the daughter turns 18. In this example, this $600 a month lasts four years. In addition, the father gets $600 a month beginning at FRA by applying for spousal benefits only before switching to his higher benefits at 70. The cumulative lifetime benefits are eventually higher in Strategy 2 than in Strategy 1 due to the higher monthly benefits after age 70.

Suppose we change the example by assuming the mother is 52, the father is 62, and the child is 14. This couple would have to weigh the merits of two scenarios: (1) the father applying for benefits at 62 so the child could receive benefits, against (2) the probable long-term reduced benefits for the younger wife after the father dies if he starts benefits at 62 instead of 70. They may opt to forego the child's benefits to ensure that the wife/mother will receive the larger $2,640 a month after his death for the rest of her life.

Living versus deceased worker: In general, a child's monthly benefit can be up to 50% of the living insured's Primary Insurance Amount or up to 75% of the deceased insured's PIA. It should be noted here there is a family maximum benefit that can be collected. This maximum is discussed in the next section of this chapter. The 50% or 75% limits mentioned here will only be applicable if the family maximum benefits limit is not breached.

Limit on benefits payable on one worker's record: The maximum family benefit payable based on one worker's record generally ranges from 150% to 180% of the worker's Primary Insurance Amount. With the exception of some workers who were in their 90s in 2010, the family maximum benefit based on one worker's record is based on bend points. In Chapter 2 we described how bend points are used to convert Average Indexed Monthly Earnings into Primary Insurance Amount.

According to the Social Security Administration's online handbook, which we do not find to be user friendly, "The family maximum is computed by adding fixed percentages of predetermined dollar amounts (i.e., the bend points) which are part of the PIA. The formula in effect for 2011 is:

Up through 972	150% of PIA
972.10 - 1403.00	1458 plus 272% of excess of 972
1403.10 - 1830.00	2630.32 plus 134% of excess of 1403.00
1830.10 or higher	3202.50 plus 175% of excess of 1830.00

"The bend points will usually change each year in the same way that the bend points used to compute the PIA change."

How are benefits split up when the family maximum benefit applies? For clarity, we assume the insured worker is a male, but the rules are parallel if the worker is female. To calculate benefits when the insured worker is alive, we first subtract his benefits and then split the remaining benefits among other beneficiaries. Furthermore, if the insured worker's ex-wife receives benefits based on his record, her benefits do not reduce the benefits payable to his current wife, children and others.

For example, assume a single father is 62 years old with a Primary Insurance Amount of $2,000 and Full Retirement Age of 66. He has three children, ages 15, 16, and 17. The father does not have sufficient earnings to affect his benefits or his children's benefits. The family maximum benefit is $3,500, calculated as:

$2,000 PIA - $1,830 from the table above = $170

($170 x 175%) + $3,202.50 from table above = $3,500 family maximum

Today at 62, the father files for benefits based on his record and receives a reduced benefit of $1,500. This reduced the maximum benefits to other family members to $1,500, the family maximum less his PIA. His children's benefits are not reduced because he began benefits early. His children each qualify for up to 50% of his PIA, or $1,000 each. If not for the family maximum, they would each receive $1,000.

The insured person – the father in this example – would not lose benefits due to the family maximum, but the beneficiaries' benefits would be adjusted. Each of the children would split the remaining $1,500 of family benefits. Each child would receive $500. Table 5.3 shows how these amounts are adjusted for the family maximum.

One year later, the oldest child turns 18 and is no longer eligible for child's benefits. The father continues to receive $1,500, and each of the two younger children now begins receiving $750 monthly, that is, they split the $1,500 maximum benefit to other family members. Although not shown in Table 5.3, one year later when the middle child turns 18 and is no longer eligible for benefits, the father will continue to receive $1,500 and the youngest child will receive $1,000 for a total of $2,500. The youngest child will not receive a higher benefit because he is only eligible for up to 50% of the father's PIA. Once the youngest child turns 18 and from that time forward, the father will continue to receive $1,500 a month in benefits.

Table 5.3.	Adjustments to Beneficiary Benefits Based on Family Maximum		
Beneficiary	**Original Benefit**	**Adjusted for the Family Maximum**	**Benefits When Oldest Child Turns 18**
Insured person	$1,500	$1,500	$1,500
Youngest child	$1,000	$500	$750
Middle child	$1,000	$500	$750
Oldest child	$1,000	$500	$0
Total	$4,500	$3,000	$3,000

Divorced Spouse's Benefits

This section is written as if the divorced spouse is a woman but, as in our other discussions, the rules are parallel for divorced men. The following information comes from "What Every Woman Should Know," with our comments appearing in parentheses. For additional associated information, go to http://www.socialsecurity.gov/pubs, and click on "What Every Woman Should Know."

"If your ex-husband is living—

"If you are divorced, you can receive benefits based on your ex-husband's work if—

- Your marriage lasted 10 years or longer;
- You are unmarried;
- You are age 62 or older;
- The benefit you are entitled to receive based on your own work is less than the benefits you would receive on your husband's work; and
- Your ex-husband is entitled to Social Security retirement or disability benefits.

"If he has not applied for benefits, but can qualify for them and is age 62 or older, you can receive benefits on his work if you have been divorced from him for at least two years."

[If she applies for benefits before FRA and her ex-husband is at least 62, whether or not he has filed for benefits, then her application will be deemed to be an application for both her own retirement benefits and spousal benefits. Similarly, if he is at least 62 and thus could file for his benefits, then if she is at least FRA she can make a restricted application for spousal benefits only based on his earnings record.]

"If your ex-husband is deceased, you can receive benefits—

- At age 60, or age 50 if you are disabled, if your marriage lasted at least 10 years, and you are not entitled to a higher benefit on your own record. [Notice that if you remarry after age 60, or age 50 if disabled, you may still be eligible for *survivor's benefits* based on the worker's record.]

- At any age if you are caring for his child who also is your natural or legally adopted child and younger than 16 or disabled and entitled to benefits. Your benefits will continue until the child reaches age 16 or is no longer disabled. You can receive this benefit even though you were not married to your ex-husband for 10 years."

The divorced wife's survivor's benefits would be the same as for a current wife. If she is Full Retirement Age for survivor's benefits or older, she is entitled to 100% of the deceased ex-husband's benefit amount. If she is between 60 and FRA, she is entitled to between 71.5% and 100% of his benefit amount, where the reduction is prorated between 71.5% and 100% based on her age. A disabled divorced wife aged 50 through 59 is eligible for 71.5% of his benefit amount. His benefit amount refers to his benefit level including reduction in benefits for beginning benefits before attaining FRA or delayed retirement credits for delaying the start of benefits until after attaining FRA.

Furthermore,

- The amount of benefits a divorced wife is eligible to collect has no effect on the amount of benefits the ex-husband and his current wife may receive.

- The earnings test applies to benefits received by a divorced spouse.

- If the divorced spouse will also receive a pension based on work not covered by Social Security, such as government or foreign work, then her Social Security spousal benefits or survivor's benefits may be affected.

Pensions from Work Not Covered By Social Security

Individuals who receive a pension from work not covered by Social Security will have their Social Security benefits reduced. These individuals include police officers, firefighters, teachers as well as employees of federal, state, or local government agencies. The **Windfall Elimination Provision** applies to *benefits based on the worker's earnings record* when he or she also receives pension benefits from an employer that does not withhold Social Security taxes. The **Government Pension Offset** applies to *spousal benefits or survivor's benefits* for widows and widowers. This section explains these reductions. It is important to note that estimated benefits from *Your Retirement Benefit Estimate* may substantially overstate an affected worker's projected Social Security benefits.

The Windfall Elimination Provision (WEP) may reduce Social Security benefits for "double dippers"—individuals who receive pension benefits from a retirement system other than Social Security. Suppose Nancy receives $1,800 per month in retirement benefits from the Texas Teachers' Retirement System, which is not part of the Social Security system. In addition, based on work other than as a Texas public-school teacher, she paid Social Security taxes on "substantial earnings" for 20 years or less. WEP affects her Social Security benefits when *based on her record*. As discussed in the Primary Insurance Amount section in Chapter 2, when converting her Average Indexed Monthly Earnings (AIME) on her work covered by Social Security to Primary Insurance Amount, if born in 1948 she would receive 90% of the first $761 of AIME plus 32% of the next $3,825 of AIME plus 15% of any remaining AIME. WEP reduces this

90% to 40% if she had "substantial earnings" subject to Social Security taxes for 20 years or less. If she had "substantial earnings" for 21 through 30 years then the percentage rises from 45% to 90%. If Nancy has 20 years or less of "substantial earnings" covered by Social Security, she would receive $380.50, [(90% - 40%)$761], less in Social Security benefits based on her record. For more details, see www.socialsecurity.gov/retire2/wep.htm. For a definition of "substantial earnings," click "WEP Chart" and then "substantial earnings."

The Government Pension Offset (GPO) reduces or eliminates the amount of *spousal and survivor's benefit* by two-thirds of the amount of the government pension. For example, suppose Nancy's husband, Andy, began his benefits at his FRA and receives $2,000 a month, while Nancy receives $1,800 a month in benefits from the Texas Teachers' Retirement System. Also, assume Nancy has no earnings record from work covered by Social Security. If not for her teacher's retirement, Nancy might be eligible for spousal benefits of $1,000 a month, half of Andy's benefits. But the GPO would eliminate her spousal benefits because $1,000 - (2/3)$1,800 is less than zero.

To repeat, Nancy's survivor's benefits are also affected by the GPO. After Andy's death, Nancy would qualify for survivor's benefits. If not for her teacher's retirement, Nancy would receive $2,000 a month from Social Security if Andy began benefits based on his record at his FRA. But the GPO would reduce this benefit amount to $800, [$2,000 − (2/3)$1,800]. An example later in this chapter explains how her monthly benefit level would be determined after Andy's death if she had an earnings record from work covered by Social Security. For further details, see www.socialsecurity.gov/pubs/10007.html.

Next, we present two examples of how a pension from work not covered by Social Security would affect Social Security benefits. Generally, the software tool and this book do not claim to provide advice for individuals with non-covered pensions. However, we do provide the prior two examples and two additional examples that should help such individuals work through their claiming options.

Example 1: Amanda is single, age 62, and has an FRA of 66. She receives a pension from work not covered by Social Security. In addition, she has 20 years or less of "substantial earnings" from work covered by Social Security and a PIA of $1,200. She turns 62 in 2011. Her monthly benefits (in today's dollars) if she starts benefits at her FRA will be $818, [$1,200 - $372], because the Windfall Elimination Provision will reduce her benefits by $372. As explained in Chapter 2, there is a formula that translates Amanda's Average Indexed Monthly Earnings (AIME) into her Primary Insurance Amount. Due to her non-covered pension and 20 years or less of "substantial earnings," Amanda will only receive 40%, instead of 90%, of the first $744 of AIME. (See www.socialsecurity.gov/retire2/wep-chart.htm for more information including the maximum reduction amount. Click on "substantial earnings" to see the minimum earnings levels by year that constitutes "substantial earnings.")

If Amanda starts benefits at age 62, she will receive 75% of $818 instead of 75% of the unreduced $1,200. Similarly, if she delays the start of benefits until age 68 or 70, she will get, respectively, 16% or 32% more than $818 per month. Said another way, the reduction in benefits and delayed retirement credits are based on the adjusted amount of $818, not on the unadjusted amount of $1,200. However, the breakeven ages are the same for Amanda as for another single retiree who does not receive a pension from work not covered by Social Security.

Example 2: Marilyn is a retired teacher with a monthly pension of $2,100 from work not covered by Social Security. In addition, she has 20 years or less of "substantial earnings" from work covered by Social Security and has a Primary Insurance Amount of $800. (See www.socialsecurity.gov/retire2/wep-chart.htm for more information. Click on "substantial earnings" for minimum earnings levels by year to constitute "substantial earnings.")

Marilyn's husband Mario has a Primary Insurance Amount of $2,000. They were both born in 1947 and have FRAs of 66. Table 5.4 presents two of their claiming strategies. It assumes Marilyn will live until age 90 and Mario until age 80. It also assumes that they each receive benefits starting in January. All dollar amounts are expressed in today's dollars.

Table 5.4.	Couple with Pension from Work Not Covered by Social Security				
Ages	Strategy 1 Marilyn's Benefits	Strategy 1 Mario's Benefits	Strategy 2 Marilyn's Benefits	Strategy 2 Mario's Benefits	Difference (in cumulative benefits)
66	$419	$2000	$419	$209	-$21,492
67	419	2000	419	209	-42,984
68	419	2000	419	209	-64,476
69	419	2000	419	209	-85,968
70	419	2000	419	2640	-78,288
71	419	2000	419	2640	-70,608
72	419	2000	419	2640	-62,928
73	419	2000	419	2640	-55,248
74	419	2000	419	2640	-47,568
75	419	2000	419	2640	-39,888
76	419	2000	419	2640	-32,208
77	419	2000	419	2640	-24,528
78	419	2000	419	2640	-16,848
79	419	2000	419	2640	-9,168
80	600		1240		-1,488
81	600		1240		6,192
...	...		...		...
88	600		1240		59,952
89	600		1240		67,632

Marilyn and Mario were born in 1947. Marilyn receives a pension from work not covered by Social Security system of $2,100 a month. In addition, she has 20 years or less of "substantial earnings" from work covered by Social Security and a PIA of $800. Mario has a PIA of $2,000. In Strategy 1, they both begin benefits at 66. In Strategy 2, she begins benefits at 66 based on her earnings record and he begins spousal benefits at that time. At 70, he switches to benefits based on his earnings record. Marilyn's benefits based on her earnings record are reduced by the Windfall Elimination Provision, while her survivor's benefits are reduced by the Government Pension Offset. The Strategy columns show monthly totals, while the Difference column shows cumulative benefits of Strategy 2 less cumulative benefits of Strategy 1. A positive value indicates that Strategy 2 has the higher cumulative benefits, while a negative value indicates that Strategy 1 has the higher cumulative benefits.

In claiming Strategy 1, they both begin benefits at age 66. If not for her pension, Marilyn would receive $800 a month. As explained in this chapter, the Windfall Elimination Provision would reduce her monthly benefits *based on her earnings record*. In this case, her benefits would be reduced by $380.50, which, after rounding down, would reduce her benefits level to $419 a month. The website listed in Example 1 provides maximum reduction amounts by year of birth. Mario would receive $2,000 a month in benefits at age 66. After his death, Marilyn would receive survivor's benefits. If not for her pension, Marilyn would receive $2,000 a month. However, the Government Pension Offset (GPO) affects her *spousal and survivor's benefits*. Her pension reduces her survivor's benefits by two thirds of her $2,100 monthly pension. The $2,000 is separated into her own benefit amount of $419 plus survivor's benefits of $1,581. Her survivor's benefits are reduced to $181 = $1,581 − (2/3)$2,100. So, Marilyn would receive $600 monthly, that is, $419 (her own benefits) + $181 (survivor's benefits) a month after Mario's death.

In Strategy 2, Marilyn begins benefits based on her record at 66 and Mario delays benefits based on his earnings record until age 70. Beginning at 66, she receives $419 a month based on her record, and Mario files for spousal benefits only of half that amount or $209 after rounding down to the nearest dollar. When Mario turns 70, he switches to benefits based on his record of $2,640 a month. After his death, Marilyn receives survivor's benefits, which are based on Mario's benefits of $2,640. If not for her non-covered pension, she would receive $2,640 a month. But her pension reduces her survivor's benefits by two-thirds of her $2,100 monthly pension. The $2,640 is separated into her own benefit amount of $419 (her own Social Security benefit) plus survivor's benefits of $2,221. Her survivor's benefits are reduced to $821, that is, $2,221 − (2/3)$2,100. So, Marilyn would receive $1,240 monthly, $419 (her own benefits) + $821 (survivor's benefits).

A key lesson from this example is that it still pays for Mario to delay the start of his benefits until age 70. By so delaying, he increases their combined monthly benefit amount by $640, and this $640 continues for their joint life expectancy. That is, after Mario's death, Marilyn receives an additional $640 a month in Strategy 2 compared to Strategy 1, an amount that lasts for the rest of her life. In addition, Mario receives spousal benefits from age 66 through 69. In this example, the additional $640 a month for his delaying benefits based on his earnings record until age 70 was not affected by the GPO. In Strategy 2, her survivor's benefits were $821 or $640 above the $181 in survivor's benefits in Strategy 1. It is frequently (but not always) the case that survivor's benefits will increase by the full amount of the delayed retirement credit, in this case by $640. So, it often pays for the higher earner with a spouse who receives a pension from non-covered work to delay his benefits until age 70. That is, frequently Lesson 2 still applies: Since at least one spouse lives well beyond the age that the higher earner turns 80, the couple's cumulative lifetime benefits will be higher if the higher earner delays benefits based on his record until age 70.

Disability Benefits

Two Social Security programs pay disability benefits: the Social Security disability insurance program and the Supplemental Security Income (SSI) program. For information about the Social Security disability program, see http://www.socialsecurity.gov/pubs/10029.html#part1. This program makes payments to individuals who cannot work because they have a medical condition that is expected to last at least one year or result in death. The SSI program makes monthly payments to people who have low income and few resources and are age 65 or older, blind, or disabled. For information about the SSI disability program for adults, see http://www.socialsecurity.gov/pubs/11000.html.

Detailed Rules You Should Know

Several times we've mentioned the volume of regulations that are part of the Social Security system. We've chosen to include the following rules that, while not applicable to everyone, are significant to the clients they do impact. The earnings test must be clearly understood by clients who desire to continue working in retirement but are considering filing for benefits before FRA. Likewise, there are certain timing issues built into the regulations that may impact claiming strategies for clients. And while the do-over option has been severely curtailed, there may be clients who will benefit from this option under its new guidelines. Our discussions and examples of these rules will prove beneficial as you develop claiming strategies for clients impacted by these details.

Earnings Test

Monthly Social Security benefits may be reduced or eliminated due to the earnings test. The earnings test is not a tax. Rather, it is a direct reduction in benefits and applies to individuals who begin receiving payments before reaching Full Retirement Age. In years before reaching FRA, Social Security benefits are reduced by $1 for every $2 of earned income above $14,160 (in 2011). In the year someone reaches FRA, benefits may be reduced by $1 for every $3 of earned income above $37,680 (in 2011). After reaching FRA, individuals can receive full benefits with no limit on earnings.

As an example, suppose Mary begins receiving Social Security benefits when she turns 62 in January 2011 and is entitled to $1,000 a month ($12,000 for the year). She told the Social Security Administration that she expects to earn $30,000 in 2011, which is $15,840 over the earnings limit of $14,160. Social Security would withhold $7,920 ($1 for every $2 earned over the limit). To do this, the Social Security Administration would withhold all benefit payments from January 2011 to August 2011. Beginning in September 2011, Mary would receive her $1,000 monthly benefit for the remainder of the year. In January 2012, she will be paid the additional $80 withheld in August 2011.

Let's change the example. Suppose Mary is 65 at the beginning of the year but reaches her FRA in October 2011. She would receive $1,000 a month in benefits before the earnings test. She told the Social Security

Administration that she expects to earn $45,000 from January through September—the month before reaching FRA. She would have $2,440 of benefits withheld ($1 for every $3 earned through September above the $37,680 limit). To do this, Social Security Administration would withhold all benefit payments from January 2011 to March 2011. Beginning in April 2011, Mary would receive her $1,000 benefit and this amount would be paid to her each month for the remainder of the year. In January 2012, she will be paid the additional $560 withheld in March 2011. For more information, see "How Work Affects Your Benefits," at www.socialsecurity.gov/pubs/10069.html.

What income counts? The earnings test is based on earned income, which includes wages, salary, and self-employment income. It does not include interest income, dividends, capital gains, withdrawals from a 401(k), 403(b), traditional IRA, Keogh and other tax-deferred pensions, or withdrawals from non-qualified tax-deferred annuities.

Adjustments that may offset benefits lost due to earnings test: Benefits lost due to the earnings test are not necessarily permanently lost. Let's continue with the prior example. Suppose Mary's Primary Insurance Amount was $1,333 when she began benefits at age 62 and zero months. Her $1,000 monthly benefit level reflects the reduction for beginning benefits 48 months before she attained FRA. Furthermore, suppose Mary loses all benefits for 10 months and had two other months with a partial reduction in benefits due to the earning test from age 62 until attaining her FRA. Once she attains her FRA, the Social Security Administration adjusts her benefits as if she began Social Security at age 63 years and zero months, twelve months after she actually began benefits, where twelve reflects the number of months in which she lost full or partial benefits. Her new monthly benefit level would be $1,066, which reflects a 36 month reduction period. *If*, again if, Mary lives to an average life expectancy of about 80 years, the additional $66 from her Full Retirement Age until her death would approximately offset the 12 months of lost benefits before she attained her FRA. Thus, the reduction in benefits is not necessarily permanently lost.

Earnings test applies to all Social Security benefits: The earnings test applies to all Social Security benefits whether these benefits are based on the worker's earnings record or a spouse's earnings record. Spousal benefits and survivor's benefits are based on a spouse's earning record and were discussed in Chapter 4. For example, Joe and Betty are married and both work. Joe receives his own retirement benefits and Betty receives her own retirement and spousal benefits. Joe's earnings could affect his own retirement benefits and Betty's spousal benefits because they are based on Joe's work record, but not Betty's retirement benefits. Betty's earnings could affect her retirement benefits and her spousal benefits but not Joe's retirement benefits. If Joe is deceased then Betty's earnings could affect her retirement benefits and her survivor's benefits.

Do-Over Option

Prior to late 2010, a provision in the Social Security rules allowed someone receiving benefits to repay all prior benefits received and start benefits anew either at that time or a later date. On December 8, 2010, the Social Security Administration dramatically curtailed this option and applied the following rules.

First, the restrictions apply only to applications for withdrawal requests for retirement benefits. They do not apply to withdrawal requests for survivor's or disability benefits. The new regulations:

- "Establish a 12-month time limit from the first month of entitlement for a withdrawal or retirement benefits request,"

- "Allow one withdrawal per lifetime, and"

- "Limit the voluntary suspension of benefits for purposes of receiving delayed retirement credits to months for which the number holder has not received a payment."

The rules represent a significant change in policy. They appear to allow the following. Individuals are allowed one opportunity per lifetime to request a withdrawal of benefits; however, that request must be within 12 months of the first entitlement month. Assume Joe applies for benefits at age 63 years and zero months and is first entitled to benefits in January 2010. If he has not previously applied for a withdrawal of benefits, he can request a withdrawal of benefits provided it is made within the 12-month time limit.

Suppose someone with an FRA of 66 began receiving benefits at age 66 years and eight months. If he had not previously applied for a withdrawal of benefits then, within one year, he could voluntarily suspend benefits. If he suspends benefits at 67 years and zero months, the suspension of benefits would begin the next month, but he would not receive delayed retirement credits for the six months—from age 66 years and eight months through 67 and zero months. This loss of delayed retirement credits would permanently reduce his eventual monthly benefit level by 4 percent.

In addition, there are potential adverse tax consequences associated with this do-over option. Suppose Jane begins benefits at age 62 in May 2011 and applies for a withdrawal of benefits request in March 2012. For tax purposes, benefits repaid in 2012 for benefits in that year are treated as if they never happened. But Jane may have paid taxes on Social Security benefits received in May through December 2011. Once these benefits are repaid in 2012, she has options for adjusting for the taxes paid on 2011 Social Security benefits. If repayments for 2011 exceed $3,000, they would be treated as either (1) a miscellaneous itemized deduction not subject to the 2% floor, or (2) a §1341 tax credit. Let's consider each tax treatment.

Suppose Jane's 2011 benefits totaled $8,000. She could write off this amount as a miscellaneous itemized deduction not subject to the 2% floor. But she may have taken the standard deduction, in which case this option may not be appropriate.

A second alternative is the tax credit. This tax credit requires that Jane recalculate her 2011 tax returns as if she did not receive Social Security benefits that year. She could claim a 2012 tax credit, a reduction in the final 2012 tax bill, on the difference between 2011 taxes that were paid and those that would have been paid if she had not received Social Security benefits. She may not be able to calculate this amount, at least not with ease. Even if her tax advisor could calculate this amount, the cost of the professional fee would perhaps offset any gain she would receive from the do-over option.

This change in the do-over option means that, for a retiree, the decision as to when to begin benefits is more important than ever. Before this change, benefits could be repaid and begun anew at a higher level. Now that this flexibility will be greatly curtailed, it is critical to select the best claiming strategy before beginning benefits.

Taxation of Social Security Benefits

Many people are not familiar with the taxation of Social Security benefits. If Social Security is a client's only income, benefits will not be taxable. But if a client has other income such as pension income, withdrawals from 401(k) or other tax-deferred account, or investment income, taxes may be owed on up to 85% of Social Security benefits.

The taxable portion of Social Security benefits can be calculated in two steps. First, calculate the **Provisional Income** (a.k.a., **Combined Income**). Provisional Income is the sum of three amounts. For most people, the first amount is the sum of wages, taxable interest, realized capital gains, and other income included in Adjusted Gross Income (except the taxable portion of Social Security benefits). This amount is called the **Modified Adjusted Gross Income** or MAGI. The other two amounts are one-half of the Social Security benefits and tax-exempt interest.

The second step is to convert Provisional Income into the taxable portion of Social Security benefits. There are two threshold amounts in this conversion. They are $25,000 and $34,000 for singles, heads of households, and qualified widow(er)s with a dependent child. The threshold amounts are $32,000 and $44,000 for couples filing jointly.

The taxable portion of Social Security is the minimum of three amounts:

1. 85% of Social Security benefits;

2. 50% of benefits plus 85% of Provisional Income beyond the second threshold amount; or

3. 50% of Provisional Income beyond the first threshold plus 35% of Provisional Income beyond the second threshold amount.

For most clients, the first or third formula will produce the lowest taxable amount. For these clients, Social Security benefits are tax free if Provisional Income is below the lower threshold amount. For each dollar of Provisional Income between the first and second thresholds, $0.50 of Social Security benefits will be taxed. For each dollar of Provisional Income above the second threshold, $0.85 of benefits will be taxed until the maximum taxable portion of 85% of Social Security benefits is taxed.

Timing Issues Affecting Eligibility for and Timing of Payments

Date Issues: There are four key, and sometimes confusing, principles in these date issues.

1. The Social Security Administration considers someone to *attain* an age the day before his or her birthday.

2. Except for age 62 and 0 months, you become eligible *for* benefits the month that you *attain* that age.

3. Special rules apply to the first month of eligibility for Social Security benefits. To be eligible *for* benefits at age 62 and 0 months, you must have *attained* that age for the entire month.

4. Benefits *for* a month are always paid the following month.

To illustrate these principles, we use examples for people born in February 1949, but the same principles apply for people born in other months.

The same answers apply to anyone born from February 3 through February 28th, the last day of the month.

Let's first consider someone born on February 3, 1949. According to the principles above, Bob attains age 62 on February 2, 2011; that is, he attains age 62 in February 2011. He attains age 62 and 1 month in March 2011, age 62 and 2 months in April 2011, and so on. He attains Full Retirement Age of 66 in February 2015, and age 70 in February 2019. Therefore, Bob would be eligible for benefits associated with someone aged 62 and 1 month in March 2011, aged 62 and 2 months in April 2011, aged 66 in February 2015, and aged 70 in February 2019.

The rules are different for someone applying for benefits at age 62 and 0 months. The earliest Bob is eligible for benefits is the first month for which he has attained age 62 for the entire month. Since Bob *attained* age 62 on February 2, the first month in which he will have attained age 62 for the entire month is March 2011. The earliest he can apply for benefits is March 2011, and his benefit level will be that associated with being 62 years and 1 month. His reduction period will be 47 months, from March 2011 until January 2015, the month before he attains FRA.

Let's look at a different example. Sandy was born on February 2, 1949, and attains age 62 on February 1, 2011. Since she is eligible for benefits for the entire month of February, the earliest Sandy is eligible for benefits is February 2011 and her benefit level will be that associated with being 62 years and 0 months. Her reduction period will be 48 months, from February 2011 until January 2015, the month before she attains FRA.

Still, here is another example in the application of these date principles. Larry was born on February 1, 1949, and attains age 62 on January 31, 2011. The first month Larry is eligible for benefits is February 2011, the first month in which he will have attained age 62 for the entire month. Larry attains age 62 and 1 month in February 2011. So, his benefit level will be that associated with someone age 62 years and 1 month. His reduction period will be 47 months, from February 2011 until December 2014, the month before he attains FRA.

In summary, with the exception of age 62 years and 0 months, some-one can begin benefits *for* a month in the month he or she *attains* that age. This statement applies to benefits based on his or her earnings record, spousal benefits, and survivor's benefits. The exception is when someone applies for benefits at age 62 (and 0 months). Someone born on the first or second of a month is first eligible for benefits that month. Everyone else is first eligible for benefits *for* the next month, when he or she attains age 62 and 1 month. Benefits *for* a month are always paid the next month.

In the text, we often say someone with an FRA of 66 would have a 25% reduction for beginning benefits at age 62. This is true for someone born on the 2nd of a month. Others are not eligible for benefits until the month they attain age 62 and 1 month, and their benefit levels are slightly higher. We leave this discussion of details to this section, and do not al-ways discuss it in the text.

We adjusted the software tool to reflect the Social Security Administra-tion's convention that someone attains an age the day before his or her actual birthday. Nothing must be done to accommodate this strange convention.

Death and Benefits: Suppose John and Karen are married and both are over 70. John and Karen are receiving $2,500 and $2,000 a month re-spectively in Social Security benefits. To be eligible for benefits, they must be alive for the full month. So, if John dies on November 30th, he would not receive benefits *for* November but Karen would receive $2,500 as a survivor's benefit *for* November. If he dies on December 1st, John would receive $2,500 and Karen $2,000 *for* November, but these amounts would actually be *paid* in December.

Retroactive Filing: The Social Security Administration allows indi-viduals to file for retroactive benefits in some instances. For example, it allows individuals to backdate the starting month for their own benefits or spousal benefits up to six months, as long as the backdating does not take them back to before their Full Retirement Age. Someone eligible for survivor's benefits can backdate their starting month by one month. So a recent widow(er) should not delay long before determining whether it is in her (his) best interest to file as soon as possible for survivor's benefits.

Children who are eligible for Social Security benefits may file for retroactive benefits for periods beginning up to six months earlier. Finally, individuals, whether single or married, can file and suspend their benefits at FRA. Then before they begin benefits, they can retroactively reinstate benefits to the month they filed (but not before FRA) and receive payment of the benefits held in suspension.

For example, Jose is single and estimates he has a long life expectancy. So, at his Full Retirement Age, Jose files for benefits and immediately suspends them with the expectation of delaying his Social Security benefits until 70. Three years later, something happens that dramatically reduces his life expectancy. He can claim his three years of suspended benefits, and the monthly benefit he will receive is equal to his Primary Insurance Amount. With this file-and-suspend strategy, he can reduce, but not eliminate, the risk of delaying benefits and dying early.

Summary

In this chapter, we discussed nontraditional, but not uncommon, situations. We also discussed children's benefits and how they can impact a parent's claiming strategy. We presented information regarding benefits for a divorced spouse. We discussed the impact to Social Security benefits for people with a pension from work not covered by the Social Security system, and we offered resources for investigating disability benefits paid by the Social Security Administration. Finally, we provided information about other rules important in crafting strategies for some clients: the earnings test, the do-over option, taxation of Social Security benefits, and timing issues.

While financial advisors may see only a few of these nontraditional situations in their practices, it is important to be familiar with the provisions that could affect benefits in these situations. These situations become complicated quickly. However, because benefits payable to children and survivors, in particular, are typically paid out when families are financially vulnerable, it is important that you guide clients in selecting the best possible strategy for their situation.

CHAPTER 6 Summary and Perspective

We wrote this book to help you craft optimal Social Security claiming strategies for clients, or for yourself if you are not an advisor. In addition, we hope it's clear the material difference that alternative strategies can make not only in cumulative lifetime benefits, but also in the longevity of a retirement savings portfolio. Yes, the rules governing Social Security benefits are complex and overwhelming. But we've simplified them into a set of lessons that will allow you to create a couple of good strategies for clients to consider. You can discuss the relative advantages and disadvantages of these smart strategies, so the clients can compare and select the claiming strategy that best fits their risk-return preferences. In this chapter, we summarize the important aspects of the book and offer a brief discussion of Social Security planning as an important part of comprehensive retirement planning.

Summary

While it is important to have an understanding of the rules and policies of the system, our goal is that you can utilize the key lessons of this book to help clients select a smart claiming strategy. Much of this book is quite technical and academic, a fitting requirement to decipher and communicate the overwhelming rules of the Social Security system. We've attempted to assimilate those rules into a set of strategies and lessons that financial advisors can use with clients in retirement income planning.

To recap the book, following the Introduction chapter, Chapter 2 defined important Social Security terms including Full Retirement Age (FRA) and Primary Insurance Amount (PIA).

Chapters 3 and 4 are arguably the most important material in this book and the Social Security claiming process. In Chapter 3, we focused on single individuals and presented strategies for deciding when to begin Social Security benefits. We explained that there are two criteria single individuals (and couples) should use when deciding when to begin benefits. The first is to maximize expected cumulative lifetime benefits and the second is to minimize longevity risk, that is, the risk that savings will be exhausted during retirement. We presented Lesson 1, a key point in Social Security claiming strategy:

Lesson 1	If a single individual lives to age 80, the cumulative lifetime benefits will be approximately the same whether benefits begin at 62, 63, 64, or any age through 70.

The bottom line of Chapter 3 is that each single individual should consider his or her life expectancy and the relative importance of the two criteria. Initially, many clients will think the sole criterion for deciding when to begin benefits is to maximize expected cumulative lifetime benefits (or the present value of lifetime benefits, a closely related criterion). But financial advisors must help clients understand that their claiming strategy also affects their portfolio's longevity. Once understood, clients can rationally select the claiming strategy that will best fit their risk-return preferences.

In Chapter 4, we presented strategies for couples who are deciding when to begin Social Security benefits. This is the longest chapter and the most difficult material in this book. While strategies for married couples are more complex than strategies for singles, there is also greater opportunity to add value by helping couples select their claiming strategy. This chapter began with explanations of spousal benefits and survivor's benefits because these benefits are often keys when deciding on a couple's claiming strategy. In addition, we presented two important concepts in Lessons 2 and 3:

Lesson 2	The relevant life expectancy for the decision of when the spouse with the higher PIA should begin benefits based on his earnings record is the lifetime of the second spouse to die, while the relevant life expectancy for the decision as to when the spouse with the lower PIA should begin benefits based on her record is the lifetime of the first spouse to die.
Lesson 3	If at least one spouse lives well beyond the age the higher earner turns 80, the couple's cumulative lifetime benefits will usually be highest if the higher earner delays benefits based on his record until reaching age 70.

Combining Lessons 1, 2 and 3 provided the basis for understanding when each partner should begin benefits.

In Chapter 4, we presented several examples to illustrate that a couple's claiming strategy is important. Indeed, the best claiming strategy may add several hundred thousand dollars in lifetime benefits. The examples also illustrated Lessons 2 and 3, and explained key insights determining when each partner should begin Social Security benefits. Further, we included a detailed example for each of four couples groups, where each couples group is defined based on the ratio of the partners' low-to-high Primary Insurance Amounts. For each group, we compared cumulative lifetime benefits of several claiming strategies for various combinations of lifetimes of each partner. Finally, we described recommended strategies for a surviving spouse after the death of his or her partner.

In Chapter 5, we discussed nontraditional situations including children who are eligible for benefits based on a parent's work record, the treatment of pensions from work not covered by Social Security, and disability benefits. While these situations are nontraditional, it's important to understand the impact to benefits on affected clients. In addition, this chapter explained details of related rules including the earnings test, the do-over option, taxation of benefits, and timing issues that affect eligibility for and timing of Social Security payments.

A financial advisor, with the aid of the recommended strategies in this book, can quickly focus a client's attention on a few good strategies and can point out the relative advantages and disadvantages of each strategy. However, to reemphasize a point made earlier, each client (whether a single individual or couple) should consider two criteria when deciding when to begin benefits: (1) maximizing cumulative lifetime benefits and (2) minimizing longevity risk. Since two criteria are involved and each client must determine the relative importance of each, it is impossible for the financial advisor to determine a client's optimal strategy. Rather, each client must make this determination.

The decision of when to begin benefits is clearly important. The difference can materially affect a client's standard of living throughout retirement. Moreover, it has clearly been a decision on which clients have had little advice, and even less advice that is good. This book and the accompanying software tool will alleviate this deficiency.

We've shown you how to craft strategies without the aid of software. But bear in mind, we've established that the rules for Social Security are intricate and voluminous. And because an appropriate strategy is critical to clients and their overall retirement income, we would be remiss if we did not point out the value of an automated tool. Crafting strategies well will require complex and multiple permutations analyzing large amounts of data. Our software tool recommends a smart strategy for each client's unique situation. In addition, it allows you to create alternative claiming strategies and to form side-by-side comparisons that will allow you and the client to make an informed choice among smart claiming strategies.

Finally, we note again that the recommended strategies in this book and the software tool are based on the current promises of the Social Security system. As was mentioned early in this book, there are no guarantees that benefits will not be changed for those aged 55 and older.

However, we believe this book and the software tool are most applicable to this age group. And we suspect that adjustments to benefits, if any, borne by this group would be modest.

Perspective

The focus of this book has been Social Security planning. Although it is only one element of a retirement plan, it is a key component and one on which financial advisors have placed too little attention. As this book has explained, the rules governing Social Security benefits are complex. But the value added of a carefully crafted Social Security claiming strategy can be significant. Due to the dismal stock market returns of 2000-2009 and generally low retirement savings rates, Social Security planning will become a more important component of retirement planning as retirees rely more on the income Social Security provides.

Retirement planning is important. Research from The Hartford's Investment and Retirement Survey in December 2009 indicated that retirees who had a formal plan were more optimistic. The research concluded that, "Those who have planned for retirement are three times more likely to be confident that they will have sufficient income in retirement as compared to those who have not planned." Furthermore, it concluded, "Those who have taken the time and expended the energy to plan for retirement or their financial future not only are in a better place financially but have a more positive outlook about their retirement future than those who have not."[13] The same statements can be applied to Social Security planning. Our experiences indicate that clients who have received Social Security planning advice are more confident that they will have sufficient income in retirement and a more positive outlook about their retirement future.

There are both financial and emotional benefits to Social Security planning. The financial benefits may include higher lifetime benefits and protection from the risk of outliving financial resources. Emotional benefits include the peace of mind that comes from knowing that the claiming

13 Investment and Retirement Survey, The Hartford, 2009.

strategy has been carefully crafted and is appropriate for the client's circumstances. Ideally, advisors should devote the same attention to Social Security planning as they do on the investment side of managing and structuring retirement assets. What has been lacking are tools that help advisors provide quality Social Security planning advice. We believe this book and the complementing software tool serve this need. As we have demonstrated throughout this book, selecting a smart claiming strategy can add hundreds of thousands of dollars in clients' cumulative lifetime benefits and minimize the probability that they will run out of money in their lifetime.

Financial planning for a retiree is more complex than planning for a client in the accumulation phase. If a pre-retiree makes a mistake, they likely have time to recover. In contrast, retirees do not have this luxury. The same statement applies to planning for Social Security. Due to recent changes in regulations, there is limited opportunity for a client to undo the choice of a poor claiming strategy. And a poor claiming strategy can adversely affect a single person for the rest of his or her life or a couple for the rest of their joint lives. Prudent retirement planning requires that they be given advice on how to create a smart Social Security claiming strategy.

We conclude with an encouraging word and a call to action. Financial advisors have the opportunity to improve clients' lives by providing financial guidance. This is the ultimate testament of trust. But as cited in a recent Financial Literacy Center study, previous research has found that many people "lack the basic knowledge of Social Security necessary for making informed decisions about when to retire and claim benefits."[14] This book has demonstrated the complexity of determining a smart claiming strategy and supports the conclusion of this study. Many Americans find Social Security overwhelming and simply choose the easiest path—which is seldom their optimal path. Because a smart and personalized Social Security claiming strategy can mean more money and security in retirement, together we have the opportunity to improve the standard of living for millions of Americans as they prepare for retirement. With that the ultimate goal, we urge you to become a Social Security authority and share your knowledge with others.

14 "What Do People Know About Social Security," Financial Literacy Center, October 2010.

APPENDIX 1 Sources of Information

This Appendix discusses three sources that contain substantial additional information about Social Security. These include the Social Security Administration, Retiree, Inc. and its affiliate Social Security Solutions, Inc., and Boston College's *Center for Retirement Research.*

Social Security Administration: The Social Security Administration's website is www.ssa.gov. This site contains a great deal of information about Social Security and the application process. Several areas are accessible from the homepage including "Estimate your retirement benefits," "Get a form," and "Get a publication." Clicking "Get a Publication" makes downloads available for 14 broad topics including "Introduction to the Social Security Program," "Retirement Benefits," "Survivors Benefits," and "Work and Earnings" to name a few. Further, subtopics such as "How Work Affects Your Benefits," "Government Pension Offset," and "Windfall Elimination Provision," are available for download. Alternatively, clicking the "Retirement" tab near the top of the homepage will provide the same site access to publications available for download.

Social Security Administration calculators to estimate retirement benefits may be accessed from the homepage by clicking "Estimate your retirement benefits" on the left hand side. In addition, by typing "handbook" in the Search box in the upper right hand corner of the homepage, the "Social Security Handbook" can be downloaded. This file exceeds 1.4 megabytes, and we find this handbook difficult to use.

Social Security Solutions, Inc. and Retiree Inc.: Retiree Inc. is a firm specializing in tax-efficient withdrawal strategies and Social Security claiming strategies. Social Security Solutions, Inc. is an affiliated company of Retiree Inc. focused on helping retirees create Social Security claiming strategies. In addition, Social Security Solutions, Inc. develops software and education for practitioners who need analytical support to provide guidance on Social Security retirement benefits. Consumers or advisors looking for more information should go to www.SocialSecuritySolutions.com.

For information about Social Security and integrating a claiming strategy with a retiree's other retirement savings, see www.RetireeIncome.com. To access content about Social Security, click on the Learning Library tab near the top. A link to the Social Security material can be found under Retirement Topics. Content specifically related to Social Security includes research, published papers and articles, and case studies. In addition, it contains shorter educational content on topics such as Full Retirement Age, the earnings test, taxation of Social Security benefits, and claiming strategies for both couples and singles.

Of particular interest to financial advisors are the case studies. Clicking on Case Studies at the top of the Overview page allows you to read cases that demonstrate that delaying the beginning of Social Security can lengthen the longevity of a financial portfolio. The additional longevity obtained from delaying Social Security depends upon the relative sizes of the individual's or couple's wealth and Primary Insurance Amounts.

As previously discussed, everything else the same, the higher the retiree's wealth the smaller the additional longevity from delaying Social Security benefits. However, the high net worth retirees tend to have higher tax rates and more funds in separate account types (e.g., 401(k), Roth accounts, taxable accounts, and perhaps others such as non-qualified tax-deferred annuities). The more dispersed the financial portfolio among separate account types and the higher the retiree's tax rate, the greater the longevity that can be added by tax-efficiently withdrawing funds from the financial portfolio. So, low-net-worth retirees typically can add the most to their portfolio longevity by delaying the start of Social Security benefits, while high-net-worth retirees may be able to lengthen their longevity most by tax-efficiently withdrawing funds during retirement. The Social Security claiming strategy and withdrawal strategy together can usually extend the longevity of a retiree's financial portfolio by several years.

Center for Retirement Research. This Boston College *Center* is an excellent source of information on Social Security. The link to this site is www.crr.bc.edu. They provide a "Social Security Claiming Guide" that provides general advice. This colorful brochure can be quickly read despite its 26-page length. Because the intended audience is the general public, its guidance is much less specific than the guidelines provided in this book. This book requires a more detailed understanding of the Social Security system than is expected of the general public, and it provides much more specific advice than the "Social Security Claiming Guide." Nevertheless, the brochure does a good job for its intended audience. As we mentioned earlier in this book, the guide states, without qualification, "Don't start early because Social Security has money problems. ... You won't get more if you do. None of the proposals [to fix Social Security] gives you more if you claim early. If you are affected, you'll get less no matter when you claim."

The *Center for Retirement Research* also publishes "The Social Security Fix-It Book." Another colorful brochure, it is also a quick read despite its 52-page length. It discusses some of the options for fixing the Social Security system's financial shortfall. Since associates of the Center are likely candidates to serve on a Social Security reform committee, their opinions are of particular interest.

From the homepage of the *Center*'s website, click the Publications tab on the left for access to publications and studies. This section contains scores of studies on various topics. Some excellent examples include "Strange but True: Claim Social Security Now, and More Later" by Alicia H. Munnell, Alex Golub-Sass, and Nadia Karemcheva; "How Much Do Households Lose by Claiming Social Security at age 62?" by Wei Sun and Anthony Webb; and "When Should Married Men Claim Social Security Benefits?" by Stephen A. Sass, Wei Sun, and Anthony Webb.

Index